How Deployments Affect Service Members

James Hosek, Jennifer Kavanagh, Laura Miller

The research descibed in this report results from the RAND Corporation's continuing program of self-initiated independent research. Support for such research is provided, in part, by donors and by the independent research and development provisions of RAND's contracts for the operation of its U.S. Department of Defense federally funded research and development centers.

Library of Congress Cataloging-in-Publication Data

Hosek, James R.
    How deployments affect service members / James Hosek, Jennifer Kavanagh, Laura Miller.
        p. cm.
    Includes bibliographical references.
    "MG-432."
    ISBN 0-8330-3868-0 (pbk. : alk. paper)
    1. United States—Armed Forces—Recruiting, enlistment, etc. 2. United States—Armed Forces—Personnel management. 3. Deployment (Strategy) I. Kavanagh, Jennifer, 1981– II. Miller, Laura, 1967– III. Title.

UB323.H669 2006
355.1'2940973—dc22

                                                                        2005029107

The RAND Corporation is a nonprofit research organization providing objective analysis and effective solutions that address the challenges facing the public and private sectors around the world. RAND's publications do not necessarily reflect the opinions of its research clients and sponsors.

RAND® is a registered trademark.

Cover image courtesy of the Office of the Assistant Secretary of Defense, Reserve Affairs

Published 2006 by the RAND Corporation
1776 Main Street, P.O. Box 2138, Santa Monica, CA 90407-2138
1200 South Hayes Street, Arlington, VA 22202-5050
201 North Craig Street, Suite 202, Pittsburgh, PA 15213-1516
RAND URL: http://www.rand.org/
To order RAND documents or to obtain additional information, contact
Distribution Services: Telephone: (310) 451-7002;
Fax: (310) 451-6915; Email: order@rand.org

Preface

The military operations under way in Iraq and Afghanistan require more-intensive and more-prolonged use of U.S. military power than at any time since the Vietnam War. The commitment of military personnel to these countries has eclipsed the scope and duration of actions in Bosnia, Kosovo, Haiti, Somalia, and Panama. Although greater in scale at its peak, the Gulf War was brief and did not extend into a long period of peacekeeping, reconstruction, and insurgency, and it did not involve urban conflict, suicide bombers, or roadside bombs. The one-third cut in active-duty manpower at the end of the Cold War, from 2.1 million to 1.4 million in uniform, has today resulted in the need for longer and repeated deployments, especially for the Army and the Marine Corps, and these deployments have posed challenges for active-duty service members and for their families.

We undertook preparation of this monograph with the objective of offering insights into the challenges faced by active-duty service members deployed to Iraq and Afghanistan, the resiliency they and their families have shown in coping with these challenges, and the adequacy of defense manpower policy in assisting members and families. The monograph draws on the perspectives of economics, sociology, and psychology; provides a formal model of deployment and retention; reviews published work; reports on the results of focus groups conducted in each of the services; and presents findings from an analysis of survey data. The focus groups and survey data relate to the period from 2003 to early 2004. And, although the circumstances in Iraq and Afghanistan have changed markedly from that time, we believe that many of the monograph's findings and implications remain relevant.

The monograph may be of interest to the military services, the Office of the Secretary of Defense, individual service members and their families, members of Congress and their staff, and the media. It may also interest foreign militaries that have converted to a volunteer system and that want to be informed about the personnel strains caused by a high operating tempo.

This monograph results from the RAND Corporation's continuing program of self-initiated independent research. Support for such research is provided, in part, by donors and by the independent research and development provisions of RAND's contracts for the operation of its U.S. Department of Defense federally funded research and development centers.

This research was conducted within the RAND National Security Research Division (NSRD) of the RAND Corporation. NSRD conducts research and analysis for the Office of the Secretary of Defense, the Joint Staff, the Unified Commands, the defense agencies, the Department of the Navy, the U.S. Intelligence Community, allied foreign governments, and foundations.

For more information on the RAND National Security Research Division, contact the Director of Operations, Nurith Berstein. She can be reached by email at Nurith_Berstein@rand.org; by phone at 703-413-1100, extension 5469; or by mail at RAND, 1200 South Hayes Street, Arlington VA 22202-5050. More information about the RAND Corporation is available at www.rand.org.

Contents

Figures

Tables

Summary

Recent developments in the national security environment have led to unprecedented strains on the all-volunteer force, including extended and increased frequency of deployment and exposure to nontraditional, hostile combat conditions. Personnel are sometimes deployed for 12 months, with only six months at home before their next deployment. A large percentage of personnel deployed to Iraq and Afghanistan have faced hostile fire or have seen friends and colleagues injured or killed (Hoge et al., 2004). One question on the minds of military planners is, How has the changed nature of military service affected the attitudes of service members toward the military and their reenlistment intentions? Previous research found that personnel who deployed were more likely to reenlist than were their peers who did not deploy (Hosek and Totten, 2002). However, these findings are based on data from the 1990s, when the pace and nature of deployment were different than they are today.

This monograph focuses on how more-recent deployments have affected military personnel and, perhaps, have altered their intention to stay in the military. We present a conceptual model of how deployment affects individual utility (in economics, the concept of individual well-being); review literature from several disciplines having both concepts and previous research relevant to deployment and retention (economics, sociology, and psychology); discuss the findings from focus groups exploring deployment- and work-pace–related issues; and present results from an analysis of Status of Forces Surveys of Active Duty Personnel, surveys of military personnel conducted by the Defense Manpower Data Center from March and July 2003 regarding the relationships between work hours, deployment, preparation, stress relative to one's usual level of stress, and reenlistment intention.

Conceptual Model and Literature

Economics, sociology, and psychology all have useful insights to contribute to our study, and we consider each in turn. We first present an expected-utility model of deployment and individual utility. The model assumes that the individual has preferences regarding home time, deployed time, and income including deployment pay. The model shows how the probability of deployment, expected duration of deployment, randomness of deployment length, base pay, and deployment pay affect utility. The model implies that the individual will have a preferred deployment time, and this is distinguished from the expected and actual deployment time. For some individuals, the expected deployment time might be less than preferred, and a higher-than-expected realized deployment time then produces a higher-than-expected level of utility. For others, expected deployment time is greater than preferred deployment time, and a higher-than-expected realized deployment time produces a lower-than-expected level of utility.

The model suggests that many service members probably prefer some deployment to none; consequently, members who were deployed might have realized levels of utility higher than those of members who were not deployed. Among deployed members, an unusually long deployment time would reduce their levels of utility. The model also implies that individuals prefer knowing how long they will be deployed to randomness of deployment time. The preferred mix of home time and deployed time depends on income (deployment pay can compensate for the disutility of long deployment) and on factors affecting the utility from home time over that of deployed time. Satisfaction from deployed time can be expected to depend on individual preparation, unit preparation, unit cohesion, combat/risk conditions, length of duty-day, communication with family, family support programs, length of deployment, and uncertainty about length of deployment. Satisfaction from home time might depend on length of duty-day, enjoyment from being together with one's family day to day, participation in family events (e.g., births, birthdays), the burden of household chores, the quality of housing, recreational facilities, schools, family support programs, and so forth.

Economic models of service member utility consider monetary as well as nonmonetary factors. Several studies support the argument that, to the extent that deployment increases individual utility by moving an individual closer to his or her preferred amount of deployment, deployment can have a positive effect on reenlistment rates (Hosek and Totten, 2002). A review of reenlistment research suggests that pecuniary variables (e.g., basic pay, bonuses) have a significant positive effect on reenlistment (Goldberg, 2001). Other variables important to service member utility include job satisfaction, civilian wage, civilian unemployment rate, and work hours (Teplitzky, Thomas, and Nogami, 1988; Boesel and Johnson, 1984; Hosek and Peterson, 1985).

Sociological literature on deployment and reenlistment focuses on small-group dynamics and unit cohesion under deployment or combat conditions; combat motivation; the effects of various types of operations on personnel and unit morale; and the tension between military and family life for service members. Studies have shown that unit bonding and commitment to the group play a role in combat motivation and individual morale (Moskos, 1970; MacCoun, 1993) and may contribute to improved group performance (Mullen and Cooper, 1993). Thus, unit cohesion can help to explain why members might choose to reenlist despite difficult deployment or work conditions.

Studies find that combat motivation may also be determined by shared ideological commitments and the perception of a threat (Moskos, 1970; Kellet, 1982). In considering the effect of deployments for operations other than war on personnel morale, research finds commonalities between troop attitudes across combat and nonconventional (peacekeeping or humanitarian) deployments (Fussell, 1975; Herzog, 1992; Miller and Moskos, 1995). Personnel tend to express satisfaction with real-world missions, including peacekeeping and humanitarian missions, that allow them to use their skills and take on additional responsibility (e.g., Miller, 1997). However, peacekeeping missions may require a different set of expectations among service members, expectations focused less on combat and more on stabilization and international relations–building (Segal and Segal, 1993; Franke, 1997).

Finally, sociological literature on the effects of deployment analyzes the tension between family and military demands, the military and the family both being "greedy institutions" that make heavy demands for the commitment and time of individuals (Segal, 1988). Previous studies suggest that spousal attitudes toward the military are linked to service member reenlistment intentions (Bourg and Segal, 1999; Lakhani, 1995), suggesting that if the family is continually sacrificed in favor of military demands, dissatisfaction of the spouse could be a factor in the member's reenlistment decision. In these studies, perceived unit support for family issues and integration of the family into the military community appear to offset some of the negative effects of military-family tension on spouse and member retention attitudes (Bourg and Segal, 1999; Burrell, Durand, and Fortado, 2003). Although increased deployments and a higher operating tempo can increase the strain that the military places on family life, improved communication while on deployments has helped to mediate this stress to some extent (Schumm et al., 2004).

A final important body of literature is that relating stress to individual and group performance. Military personnel face a range of stressors on deployment, including physical/environmental stressors, high operating tempo and long work hours, and family separation. Previous surveys of military personnel have shown that these stressors affect the morale and performance of military personnel (Campbell et al., 1998; Halverson et al., 1995). However, research on how deployment stressors affect reenlistment is mixed, with some studies finding negative effects and others finding positive effects (Kelley and Hock, 2001; Hosek and Totten, 2002). Much research has suggested a U-shaped relationship between stress and performance—that is, individual performance is higher under moderate levels of stress than under very high and very low levels of stress (Selye, 1956).

Stress can have several effects on individual functioning relevant to the military, including perceptual narrowing (paying attention to fewer sensory cues or stimuli that could contribute to behaviors or decisions), reduced attention to important stimuli or cues, altered or abbreviated decisionmaking processes, and increased task completion time (Easterbrook, 1959; Janis and Mann, 1977; Friedman, 1981; Staw, Sandelands, and Dutton, 1981; Idzikowski and Baddeley, 1983). Stress can affect group performance by reducing communication between members, contributing to a concentration of power in the leadership ranks, and leading to poor group decisionmaking (Driskell, Carson, and Moskal, 1988; Janis and Mann, 1977; Bowers, Weaver, and Morgan, 1996).

Moderators are variables that can intervene in the stress-performance relationship and reduce the level of stress resulting from given stressors, as well as the effect of stress on individual or group functioning. Just as preferences are person-specific in the economic model of utility, stress responses are person-specific. For any person, important moderators of stress include self-efficacy beliefs, personality, individual characteristics, additional information, and unit cohesion and leadership (Pearson and Thackray, 1970; Jex and Bliese, 1999; Kahana, Harel, and Kahana, 1988; Adler, Vaitkus, and Martin, 1996; Glass and Singer, 1972); Kirmeyer and Dougherty, 1988; Griffith, 1998).

Training is another significant moderator and, perhaps, the one most relevant to the military (Driskell and Johnston, 1998; Sheehy and Horan, 2004; Hytten, Jensen, and Skauli, 1990; Friedland and Keinan, 1992; Saunders et al., 1996; Serfaty, Entin, and Johnston, 1998). Stress-exposure training, in which individuals or groups are exposed to certain types of stressors and asked to perform tasks under these stressors, is a common training technique that can help provide individuals with accurate expectations of the types of stress they might face and how they will respond under stressful conditions; teach them coping strategies to deal with stressors and challenges; and help them maintain effective performance even under difficult conditions (Kozlowski, 1998; Friedland and Keinan, 1992; Saunders et al., 1996; Serfaty, Entin, and Johnston, 1998).

Although moderate levels of stress may improve performance, long-term exposure to stressors or a single exposure to a highly traumatic stressor can have adverse health effects, including post-traumatic stress disorder and other mental health problems, both of which have affected veteran populations in the past (Adler and Castro, 2001; Adler, Vaitkus, and Martin, 1996; Litz et al., 1997a, b). Given the intense nature of combat and counterinsurgency operations in Iraq, military health officials are closely monitoring the mental health of returning soldiers and using short-term treatment (combat stress teams deployed to the field) to prevent more-widespread health consequences (Helmus and Glenn, 2005).

The model and these bodies of literature create a context for our focus-group discussions and provide support and explanations for many of the findings from our data analysis.

Findings from the Focus Groups

We conducted separate focus groups with enlisted personnel and with officers in each service in the first six months of 2004. The focus groups covered topics such as expectations of service life, expectations of deployment, most valuable military experiences, unexpected challenges, deployment experiences, suggestions for improved preparation for service life and deployments, and reenlistment or career plans. Most focus groups were enlisted personnel; most focus group members were junior or early-career personnel. Focus group members came from a variety of occupations.

Focus group members who had deployed reported many different sources of deployment stress. Preparing for deployment created stress from training, personal preparation, and family preparation. Preparation required weeks of fast-paced work and time away from family prior to the deployment itself. Increased frequency and length of deployment, long work hours, and intense work pace on deployment were cited as factors that increased personnel stress and led to burnout and exhaustion. Personnel differed on whether or not these factors would affect their reenlistment intentions. Some members reported that they enjoyed the intense work pace, finding it exciting and challenging, but most did not. Physical challenges (heat, poor sanitation, lack of supplies) and exposure to danger were also significant sources of stress for those who deployed to combat zones. Uncertainty surrounding deployment dates and job requirements also increased stress, particularly when this uncertainty concerned how to act in specific combat or peacekeeping situations. Some personnel felt that better preparation for counterinsurgency and urban combat operations would have decreased the uncertainty associated with their mission and reduced their stress. Separation from family and friends created stress for personnel. Some focus group members said separation from family was one of the hardest aspects of deployment and caused them to consider leaving the military. Others said separation was difficult, but not enough to affect their reenlistment intentions. Finally, reintegration with family and readjustment to life at home were stressors faced by personnel after returning from deployment. Although the military offered briefings and counseling services for returning personnel, focus group members had mixed feelings about their usefulness.

Personnel who did not deploy were stressed by deployments, too, because their workload and operational tempo increased. The requirements of preparing personnel for deployment and supporting the units that had already deployed increased their work hours and workweeks. Focus group members said that personnel shortages caused by the loss of personnel to deployment meant that those left behind had to accept more responsibilities and take on extra work. Overtime and longer workweeks created family-separation stress for nondeployed personnel by taking them away from their families and preventing them from taking part in family activities. Nondeployed personnel also had to deal with the stress of reintegrating with returning deployed units, which could sometimes be difficult because deployed units had formed strong bonds and had a set of shared experiences that did not include the nondeployed.

Although focus group participants reported that deployments had many negative aspects, we also heard about several benefits of deployments that improved the morale and deployment attitudes of those service members to whom we spoke. First among these was financial gain. Military personnel in our focus groups noted that special and incentive pays relating to deployment (especially Family Separation Pay, Hostile Fire Pay, and tax exemptions for money earned while deployed to combat zones) significantly increased their total compensation and helped offset some of the negative effects of deployment for them and their families. Another benefit was the opportunity, on deployment, for the member to use his or her training and preparation in real-world situations. Deployment also offered personnel the chance to take on additional responsibility and participate in challenging, fulfilling missions. In some cases, successful completion of deployed operations meant learning to handle situations and missions for which members had not been trained explicitly. Participants reported returning home with a sense of accomplishment because they had contributed to a larger cause. Finally, focus group members valued deployment for the opportunity to build strong bonds with other members of their units. They said their units became like families while on deployment, and these connections lasted when the unit came home.

Our focus group members (also referred to as *discussants*) cited several factors that moderated their stress, both while on deployment and at home base. Training was perhaps the most significant stress reducer. Discussants noted that their training helped to prepare them for the requirements of their missions and day-to-day jobs. However, some Army and Marine personnel in our groups commented that they lacked training in counterinsurgency and peacekeeping that might have been useful in reducing their stress and improving their performance. Importantly, the services are now implementing this type of training.

Discussants also cited talking with friends and colleagues as helpful in coping with their stress and dealing with traumatic or difficult experiences, preferring to rely on other members in their units for support when feeling stressed out or depressed rather than turning to chaplains or mental health professionals. They reported that it was more helpful to talk to people who had been through similar experiences, particularly combat experiences, than to a third party who might not be able to relate directly. In addition, a stigma was attached to seeking help from a mental health professional, and a permanent record of the visit would be created. Military-sponsored reintegration briefings were also cited as a somewhat helpful resource.

Overall, our focus groups suggested that deployment experiences include positive and negative aspects. For some individuals, the positive outweighed the negative; for others, the opposite was true. Individuals reported that they felt fairly well prepared to deal with and adapt to stress and challenging job requirements. Finally, focus group discussions suggest that the finding that reenlistment rates are higher among personnel who have deployed may be explained, at least in part, by both the positive effects of deployment on those who deployed and the negative effects of nondeployment on those who did not deploy.

Analysis of Survey Data

The data analysis was based on Status of Forces Surveys of Active Duty Personnel for March and July 2003 (Defense Manpower Data Center, 2003a, b). The analysis focused on stress and intention to stay in the military. However, the measures of stress available in the survey were self-reports of whether stress was higher or lower than usual, rather than an absolute metric of stress (such as a measured electric shock or a systematically varied set of purportedly threatening circumstances applied in an experimental setting) based on a specific stressor or stress-assessment instrument. The measures of intention to stay were also based on self-reports. We analyzed two measures of stress, higher-than-usual work stress and higher-than-usual personal stress; we analyzed four measures of intention—intention to stay, intention to stay for a career of 20 years or more, whether desire to stay increased in the past year as a result of being away from permanent duty station or, for those not away, as a result of not being away, and whether the respondent felt that his (or her) spouse wanted him (or her) to stay in the military. The explanatory variables included categorical variables for the number of times in the past 12 months that a member worked longer than the usual duty-day, whether the member was away from home station in the past 12 months, whether being away involved participating in combat operations in Operation Enduring Freedom (OEF) or Operation Iraqi Freedom (OIF), whether being away was longer or shorter than expected, whether the member felt prepared, and whether the member felt his or her unit was prepared. These variables corresponded closely to topics discussed by focus group members. Additional variables controlled for junior/senior rank, married/not married, female/male, and minority/nonminority.

We estimated linear probability models for the different measures of stress and intentions. Among the measures, the higher-than-usual work stress and the intention to stay told the core story; the results for the other measures were in many ways similar but showed weaker statistical relationships. Generally speaking, the explanatory variables in the higher-than-usual work stress and the intention-to-stay regressions were statistically significant.

Relationship Between Higher-Than-Usual Work Stress and Intention to Stay
Cross tabulations showed that service members who reported higher-than-usual work stress also indicated a higher intention to stay on active duty. This result can be understood in terms of the particular measure of stress and the dynamics of the military personnel system. As mentioned, the stress variable is not an absolute measure of stress but the individual's per-

ception of whether stress is higher than usual. It is possible that an absolute measure of stress would have a negative relationship with intention to stay. The positive relationship between self-reported higher-than-usual work stress and intention to stay, we suggest, reflects an internal sorting process: Service members who are well-matched to the military service may be more likely to have a positive intention to stay and to be assigned or promoted to positions that have more responsibility and that more frequently involve stress.

Given this positive relationship, we did find in the regressions that variables that increased the likelihood of higher-than-usual work stress also decreased the likelihood that the individual would stay in the military. That is, the explanatory variables typically had opposite effects on higher-than-usual work stress and intention to stay. For instance, more numerous workdays longer than the usual duty-day tended to increase our stress measure and decrease intention to stay. These effects were larger for personnel who had been away from home base in the past 12 months, because these personnel had more workdays longer than the usual duty-day. Further, personnel who reported the greatest decrease in their intention to stay over the previous 12 months were also likely to be the ones reporting a high intention to stay at survey time. Nevertheless, the simple association between higher-than-usual work stress and intention to stay remained positive: Members who reported higher-than-usual stress also had a higher intention to stay, and members who had a higher intention to stay also were more likely to report having higher than usual stress.

Regressions on Higher-Than-Usual Work Stress and Intention to Stay

As mentioned, the explanatory variables often had opposite effects on higher-than-usual work stress and intention to stay: A variable that increased the likelihood of a member reporting higher-than-usual work stress typically decreased the likelihood of intention to stay. According to the regression results,

- frequently working longer than the usual duty-day increased the probability of higher-than-usual stress and decreased the probability of intention to stay.
- personnel who were away in the past 12 months, many of whom were presumably deployed, had more instances of working longer than the normal duty-day than did personnel who were not away. This frequency contributed to higher-than-usual stress and lower intention to stay among those away than among those not away. The relationship between working longer than the usual duty-day and higher-than-usual stress was the same for personnel who were away as for those who were not away, as was that between working longer than the usual duty-day and intention to stay. Therefore, being away per se did not have a differential effect on higher-than-usual stress or intention to stay. Instead, the effect came from the fact that those away generally had more long days than did those who stayed at home base.
- involvement in OEF/OIF combat operations did not affect the probability of higher-than-usual work stress for enlisted personnel, except for airmen, for whom it decreased this stress; also, it increased Army officer stress and decreased Marine officer stress. Involvement in OEF/OIF combat operations did not affect intention to stay, except for Army enlisted and officers, for whom it was associated with a decrease.

- our measures of work stress and intention to stay were related to whether time away was less, or more, than expected. Higher-than-usual work stress was more likely and intention to stay was less likely when personnel were away much more than expected.
- higher-than-usual work stress was less likely and intention to stay was more likely if the member felt personally prepared and felt that his/her unit was well prepared.
- senior-rank enlisted personnel were less likely to have higher than usual work stress (except in the Air Force) and more likely to intend to stay, compared with junior-rank enlisted personnel. Senior-rank officers had no difference in the likelihood of higher-than-usual work stress and were more likely to intend to stay, compared with junior-rank officers.
- marital status was unrelated to higher-than-usual work stress, but had a positive effect on intention to stay. However, being married was associated with a higher likelihood of higher-than-usual personal stress.

Several of these findings supported what we heard from focus group participants. First, that deployment itself was not significantly related to higher-than-usual work stress or to intention to stay was consistent with focus group discussions. As noted above, personnel in our groups reported that deployments contained both positive and negative aspects and had generally mixed feelings about whether deployment experiences would affect their reenlistment intentions.

Second, the significance of numerous long workdays in the stress and intention-to-stay regressions reflected what we heard in our focus groups. Deployed personnel and non-deployed personnel alike noted that the increased operating tempo led to longer work hours and a more intense work pace, which increased work stress and caused some members to consider leaving the military. The relevance of preparation to higher-than-usual work stress and intention to stay supported the focus group finding about the importance of training for military personnel.

Third, the data analysis also confirmed the negative effects of uncertainty—deployment length differing from what was expected—on stress and intentions that we heard from some focus group members.

Fourth, although not recapped above, the effect of the member's deployment and long work hours on spousal attitudes, as well as the effect of time away on the likelihood of higher-than-usual personal stress, was consistent with focus group comments about the strain that deployments placed on family members and relationships.

The literature discussed above also supported the data analysis—for example, the effect of deployments on reenlistment, the relevance of an expected utility model to analyzing member preferences and intentions, the tension between work and family for military personnel, the effect of stress on job performance and morale, and the relevance of certain moderators to reducing the effects of stress.

Conclusions and Policy Implications

Taken together, our focus groups and data analysis provide insights into the effect of deployment on military personnel and permit us to draw several implications for policy.

Service members value deployments as an opportunity to use their training in real-world missions and to participate in meaningful operations. This implies that, when possible, deployments should be spread widely across qualified service members and units rather than limited to repeatedly deploying the same individuals.

Deployments often enable service members to apply their training to actual situations, assume new responsibilities, and take on challenges. This sense of accomplishment from deployments contributed to positive deployment attitudes among personnel to whom we spoke and can help explain why we found in the data analysis that deployment did not decrease intention to stay. At the time of our data, 2003 into early 2004, most active-duty personnel had been deployed to Iraq or Afghanistan once or not at all. By 2005, many soldiers and Marines had deployed, some had deployed twice, and some were facing a third deployment. The burden of deployment has been spread widely, and although the burden has been heavy, reenlistment remains high. Higher reenlistment bonuses have no doubt helped to sustain reenlistment, and we speculate that service members continue to find satisfaction in the opportunity to use their training and experience in actual missions and to meet new challenges.

Deployment pay helps to offset negative aspects of deployment. Military officials should examine additional ways to compensate personnel who are sent on long, difficult, or dangerous deployments or are deployed frequently, and they have initiatives under way to do so.

Previous research confirms the importance of pay in reenlistment decisions. Many focus group participants were clear that deployment pay was a positive aspect of deployment and one that improved their attitudes toward deployment and military service. Our deployment model indicated that, beyond some point, increases in time deployed would cause satisfaction to decrease at an increasing rate. Some focus group members said that they did not look forward to a military life that would have them deployed a large fraction of the time. The model and focus group comments suggest that increasing deployment pay depending on the member's previous amount of deployment over some period—for example, in the previous three years—could offset some of the negative effects of long and frequent deployments on morale and reenlistment. In addition, high current and future deployments may deter some prospective recruits, and the military may need to compensate for this greater perceived risk.

The services have already increased the use of enlistment and reenlistment bonuses, and, if reenlistment occurs in a combat zone, the bonus is tax-exempt. Alternatively, deployment pay could be revised to increase its flexibility and its ability to compensate members for the sacrifice of long deployments. Current deployment pays appear to be moving in this direction. For example, "Hardship Duty Pay for Involuntary Extension of Duty" is activated for members assigned or attached to specific units in the Iraqi area of operations that have been in Iraq and/or Afghanistan for 12 months within a 15-month period and have been asked to stay past the 12-month-rotation date. As an another option, the most common deployment pays—Family Separation and Hostile Duty Pays—could be restructured to pay at a higher rate for extensive deployment (meaning a large number of days away in a given period, or an unusually long deployment, or both). Furthermore, prospective recruits who might today anticipate more frequent, long, dangerous deployments than in the past may demand higher pay to compensate for being placed at greater risk. Finally, Congress has passed legislation in the National Defense Authorization Act 2004 permitting a bonus of $100 per day for members deployed over the predefined threshold of 400 days in any 730-day period or more than 191 days in a 365-day period. However, this High Deployment Pay has been suspended under Secretary of Defense authority since its formulation. Suspension probably resulted from the fact that High Deployment Pay would have reduced the services' ability to flexibly deploy personnel needed for OEF/OIF and, at the same time, would have increased the cost of military operations. Although $100 per day might not be the right amount, some sort of compensation for long deployments along these lines might be effective.

It seems worthwhile to analyze whether and how to alter the compensation structure—for example, to increase deployment pay depending on the extent of the service member's prior deployment, to use enlistment and reenlistment bonuses to offset today's higher risk of future deployment, or to increase the rate of deployment pay in order to most directly affect enlistment and reenlistment attitudes and behaviors. These questions are complex and will require further research before any concrete recommendations can be made.

It is worth considering additional pay and recognition for nondeployed personnel who are often called upon to work longer than the usual duty-day.

Many nondeployed personnel frequently worked long days to support the heightened pace of military operations. Our analysis showed that frequently working longer than the usual duty-day resulted in a higher likelihood of higher-than-usual stress and a lower likelihood of intention to stay—for both nondeployed and deployed personnel. Nondeployed service members in our focus groups commented on the long hours they had put in to accomplish their unit's assigned work, and some said that doing so created family stress and left little time for their personal life. Service members receive no additional compensation or formal recognition for frequently working longer than the usual duty-day.

It seems worth considering whether additional pay should be instituted for these individuals and what the specific terms and level of such pay would be. One option would be to extend the eligibility for Special Duty Assignment Pay, which is payable to personnel in specific jobs as defined by the Secretary of Defense, to include certain personnel who do not deploy, but who fill difficult positions at continental United States (CONUS) bases. Recognition should also be considered—for example, through a public event, commendation, or decoration.

Family separation, high tempo, long work hours, and uncertainty surrounding deployments are some of the more negative aspects of deployment and aspects that most significantly affect higher-than-usual stress and intention to stay. These aspects could be addressed through improved access to communication channels for deployed personnel, improved communication to service members about deployments, increased attention to the number of hours service members are asked to work, and, perhaps, through expanded family support programs.

Our focus group discussions and data analysis suggest that strain of deployment on family relationships, uncertainty surrounding deployment length, and long work hours are factors that increase the likelihood of higher-than-usual stress and decrease the intention to stay. Comments in our focus groups implied that effective, accessible, inexpensive communication home while on deployment could help to reduce the stress of family separation. Turning to the effects of uncertainty, a predictable rotation cycle could help to offset the adverse effects on stress and intention to stay caused by differences between expected and actual length of deployment. When deployment length is not predictable—for example, because of uncertainty about operation requirements—it would be useful to advise members of this uncertainty so that they and their families can plan around it.

Given that long work hours effect higher-than-usual stress and reduce intentions to stay, military planners should pay careful attention to why personnel are being asked to work longer than the normal duty-day so often, add personnel if possible, eliminate or postpone low-priority tasks, and examine potential ways to compensate and recognize personnel for frequently working long hours. Expanded family programs might also play a role. However, determining which programs to expand and in what way may require an assessment of the benefits and cost of such changes, including a sense of whether some families—for example, those living off base—would be better served by having more money than by expanded family programs.

Training and preparation are important to improving the ability of personnel to respond effectively in challenging or unfamiliar circumstances. They help reduce the likelihood of higher-than-usual stress and increase the intention to stay. Although existing training is extensive, the military should continue to revise and update its training programs in a timely way to address the changing nature of combat and the requirements of nontraditional combat.

The importance of training and preparation in helping personnel deal with and perform under stress is supported by the literature, data analysis, and focus group comments. Many personnel in our focus groups agreed that training prepared them to perform their duties, but many also felt that existing training needed to be revised to include more training for nontraditional, counterinsurgency, and peacekeeping operations. The military is already adapting its training, using lessons learned in Iraq. Training programs should be kept flexible and responsive, so that changes in enemy tactics can quickly be incorporated into predeployment preparation.

Many service members cope with combat-related stressors informally by turning to their peers for support. It may be worthwhile to consider ways of removing the stigma, or reluctance, to seek professional counseling and, further, to consider additional training to enable service members to be more effective in counseling or supporting one another.

Our data analysis found that involvement in OEF/OIF combat operations was often unrelated to higher-than-usual stress and intention to stay—a finding that may be a product of the time of our data, 2003 and early 2004. The results could differ in 2005, now that many more service members have been subjected to stress from insurgency attacks. Previous and very recent research on returning veterans, combined with focus group discussions about the difficulties of reintegration and readjustment, suggest that attention must be paid to the mental health consequences of high work stress and combat-intense deployments.

Military health officials and leaders are aware of this risk and are taking steps to ensure that personnel receive the counseling and support they require during and after their deployments. However, most focus group participants reported that they and their colleagues were hesitant to ask for professional help for fear of being perceived as weak or of harming their chance for promotion. They were also skeptical of the value of some existing programs, and some wished that the military would expand its existing reintegration training. Military officials should work against the conception that seeking help for combat-related mental health problems is weak or will affect a member's military career. They should ensure that support services are accessible to all returning personnel and address the most common sources and manifestations of postdeployment mental problems. The Army is currently screening returning personnel for post-traumatic stress disorder (PTSD), a process that eliminates the need for an individual soldier to decide whether to seek help and that aids in ensuring that soldiers with PTSD symptoms are referred for care. In addition, it might be useful to train soldiers in how to help other soldiers handle stress.

Further Research

Further research on the issue of how deployments affect reenlistment seems warranted. Additional analysis of more-recent Status of Forces surveys and personnel data would enable researchers and military planners to determine whether the relationships between work hours, deployments, higher-than-usual work stress, and reenlistment intentions are changing as longer, more-hostile deployments become the norm and as individuals return from their second or third tour. Interestingly, only the surveys contain information about long work hours, whereas the services' personnel files, which have been frequently used in retention analyses, do not. Future work should also revisit the question of how reenlistment bonuses and special pays affect the reenlistment of personnel with extensive deployment.

Acknowledgments

Many people contributed to our research. We wish to thank Lt. Col. Daniel Deamon, Lt. Cmdr. Mark Edwards, and Lt. Col. Chuck Armentrout for helping to arrange permissions for the focus groups that proved central to the analysis and findings of this monograph. Laura Castaneda joined us in conducting the focus groups, Meg Harrell advised us on how to code the focus group notes and write up the results, and Mark Totten assisted us in the analysis of the survey data. We are grateful to our reviewers, Sheila Kirby and Gail Zellman, who offered excellent suggestions for strengthening the quality of the monograph, and to our editor, Marian Branch. We also wish to thank Susan Everingham for her counsel and for partial funding of the research. Finally, our research would not have been possible without funding from the RAND independent research and development (IR&D) program.

CHAPTER ONE

Introduction

The U.S. military is now deployed in a magnitude and duration never before sustained with an all-volunteer force. During the Gulf War (1990–1991), 697,000 U.S. troops served in the Persian Gulf, most for less than a year.[1] About 20,000 U.S. troops deployed to Bosnia (1995–1996), and about 7,000 deployed to Kosovo (1999). The use of the military in peace operations and small-scale contingencies, as in Haiti in 1994 and Somalia in 1993, was appreciably higher in the 1990s than during the Cold War, making deployment a more expected part of military life even during periods of nominal peace. Yet, peacekeeping deployments were usually six months or less and involved small numbers of personnel. Those who deployed more than once often were sent to different parts of the world—for example, the Army's 10th Mountain Division deployed to the Southern United States for hurricane relief, followed by Somalia in Africa and Haiti in the Caribbean. Another defining feature of the Iraq/Afghanistan operations period is the number of casualties, which is higher than for any operation since Vietnam—and rising (1,900 as of September 20, 2005).

Military leaders are adapting their forces to these new circumstances, but such circumstances represent a major challenge, especially for ground forces. The fact is, the services and service members have so far met the challenge well. At present (mid-2005), active-duty retention rates are higher than the average over the past few years, despite some decrease in the past six months, and recruiting is in good shape, except for the Army, which expects shortfalls this fiscal year in the actives, Reserve, and National Guard.

Is a Manpower Challenge Indicated?

What are some indicators of the manpower challenge? Soldiers and Marines are experiencing their second and third deployments to Iraq, and it is common for units to be home only six months before deploying again. Army deployments are now typically 12 months long, and Marine deployments, about 7 months long. About 14,000 Fort Carson, Colorado, troops returned from Iraq in March and April 2004 after a year in Iraq, and half of them received orders in July 2004 to deploy to Iraq and Kuwait as soon as October (Kelley, 2004). Press coverage indicates that personnel are showing signs of being "weary of back to back deploy-

---

[1] The peak number of troops at any time was about 560,000. The buildup of forces took place in fall 1990 and early winter 1991, and forces began returning home in March 1991. See http://www.pdhealth.mil/deployments/gulfwar/background.asp#events.

ments that have separated many of them from their families for 18 of the last 24 months—deployments that threaten to continue for as far into the future as they can see" (Balzar, 2004), and that "for combat-weary Marines, each stint adds to the strain" (Zaroya, 2005).

In 2005, the Marine Corps commandant attributed a three-year trend of increasing suicide rates for enlisted Marines to the operational tempo (Tyson, 2005b). The services are also having to either absorb or discharge thousands of veterans from Iraq and Afghanistan who have physical disabilities, post-traumatic stress disorder (PTSD), or readjustment problems (Scharnberg, 2005; Welch, 2005). For the first time, the Army deployed many of its top drill sergeants and instructors from Fort Polk, Louisiana, and Fort Irwin, California, potentially harming future training and readiness (Schmitt and Shanker, 2004). In 2004, the Army notified 5,600 retired and discharged soldiers who are members of the Individual Ready Reserve that they would be recalled to active duty and possibly deployed to Iraq or Afghanistan.

The Navy is moving toward new models of deployment that alter the deployment and family-separation schedules to which sailors have become accustomed. These changes include Sea Swap, which rotates crew members to ships at sea and requires a smaller rotation base (fewer sailors in port awaiting the next deployment—i.e., less time between deployments), and the Fleet Response Plan, which reduces time between ship deployments, increases the interval between maintenance periods, and changes manpower processes to increase the readiness and deployability of the fleet. The goal of the Fleet Response Plan is to allow the fleet to sustain at least six carrier strike groups that can deploy immediately after an emergency order (surge-capable groups) and another two strike groups that can deploy within 90 days of the emergency order.

Today's sustained operations in Iraq and Afghanistan seem likely to produce a different set of expectations about military life, particularly about the occurrence, duration, and frequency of deployments. In addition, most directly relevant to the lives of soldiers is the effect of long and difficult deployments on their well-being, including individual and family stress, postdeployment readjustment, and PTSD. The concern has been that extensive deployments and their effect on personnel and their families could hurt morale, recruiting, and retention, and, therefore, that policy must be structured and implemented to guard against such possible damage.

Previous research on the relationship between deployment and retention found that troops who were deployed were more likely to remain in the service than troops who were not (Hosek and Totten, 1998, 2002). Officers who were deployed were more likely to continue in service than were nondeployed officers (Fricker, 2002). Among first-term enlistees, those who served on a deployment not involving hostile duty were most likely to remain in the military, followed by those who deployed with hostile duty, followed by nondeployed enlistees. The difference in retention between the deployed and nondeployed was even larger for second-term enlisted personnel than for first-term personnel.

But previous research focused on the end of the 1990s, when deployments were shorter, less frequent, smaller, and different in nature than current deployments. Deployments to Iraq have involved multi-unit combat, peacekeeping, nation building, and an escalating insurgency. The data in previous analyses did not contain information about the expectations and concerns of individual service members and their families; or details about the deployment, such as mission, location, equipment, resistance, success, and casualties; or the circumstances surrounding deployment, such as training, preparation, and postdeployment regeneration. Such differences led us to wonder whether the approaches and findings in previous work on the personnel effects of deployment remained apt. We also saw value in attempting to bring together several disciplinary strands, as opposed to past work that compartmentalized research along disciplinary lines.

Finding Answers and the Organization of This Monograph

The purpose of the research reported here was to gain insights into how the intense pace of current deployment affects active-duty personnel. Specifically, the key question today is, Will frequent, long, dangerous deployments increase stress, diminish morale, and, ultimately, decrease service members' willingness to stay in military service? Our research does not provide a definitive answer to that question, but it does offer information about how deployments to Iraq and Afghanistan have affected service members and about what might be done—and, in some cases, is already being done—to support service members and ensure their continued service.

The monograph is organized as follows. In Chapter Two, we present an expected-utility model of deployment and retention and review related economic, sociological, and psychological literature. In Chapter Three, we discuss the findings from focus groups we conducted in 2004 in each service, and in Chapter Four we present an analysis of 2003 survey data. In Chapter Five, we summarize the findings and discuss their implications for policy, and we briefly suggest topics for further research.

CHAPTER TWO

Research Approaches to Deployment and Retention

To answer the key question of this research, we took a multidisciplinary approach, drawing on economics, sociology, and psychology, then used the insights from these fields to help understand our findings from focus groups and the analysis of survey data.

The expected-utility model shows how home time, deployed time, pay, and other factors can be portrayed in a cohesive framework describing service members' satisfaction and willingness to stay in service. The model is a point of departure for our literature review, and we relate the literature to the model. We are aware that models based on sociology or psychology might be equally helpful and also could be good points of departure. Also, the expected-utility model is technical, and some readers may want to skip over it and move directly to its implications (several pages below) and the literature review.

We also reviewed sociological and psychological literature. The sociology studies concern group cohesion and morale; combat motivation; attitudes before, during, and after deployment; personnel responses to the demands of nontraditional operations; and stresses on the service member and his/her family. The psychology studies focus on the relationship between stress and performance—for example, what factors induce stress, how stress affects individual performance, and how preparation and training can moderate the adverse effects of stress. We also reviewed some literature on the effects of long-term exposure to stress and exposure to severe stressors—post-traumatic stress disorder (PTSD) and other maladaptive stress reactions.

Expected-Utility Model of Deployment and Retention

Individual preferences are fundamental to understanding how deployment affects a member's current level of satisfaction, or *utility,* as well as the member's willingness to continue serving in the military. Preferences differ by individual, and the model we present can be thought of as having different preferences—a different utility function—for each person, although the same factors are assumed to affect each person's utility. The model assumes that deployment occurs randomly and is outside the individual's control. Current deployment affects current utility, and the mean and variance of deployment affect the expected future utility of staying in the military and, therefore, retention intention. The purpose of the model is to offer some understanding of how deployments affect the process of deciding whether to stay in service, and it can be extended to include learning and dynamic behavior.[1]

How much deployment would the individual prefer if the individual could choose? We assumed that an individual's utility depends on income, time at home station (home time), and time away including deployment (time deployed). The fraction of the period spent at home station is $(1 - d)$, and fraction of time deployed is d. Base pay is m, and we let w be the amount of deployment pay if the individual were deployed for the entire period, wd be the deployment pay received for the fraction of the period d. Utility depends on income $m + wd$, home time $(1 - d)$, and deployment time d: $U(m + wd, 1 - d, d)$. All deployments are assumed to be of the same type, but the model can be modified to allow for different types of deployment. For instance, deployment type might depend on combat, peacekeeping, insurgency, climate, living conditions, diseases, and so forth.

Let us assume that deployment time is distributed uniformly between d_1 and d_2; that is, when deployment occurs, the length of the deployment will be d_1 or more, but no more than d_2. Let $\delta = (d_2 - d_1)/2$, so that mean deployment time, given deployment, is $\mu = d_1 + \delta$. It can be shown that the variance of deployment time, given deployment, is $\sigma^2 = \delta^2/3$.

Expected utility equals the utility when at home, which occurs with probability $(1 - p)$, plus expected utility when deployed, which occurs with probability p. *Expected utility when deployed* is an average of the utility at each deployment length times the likelihood of that length. For a uniform distribution, the probability density equals $1/(2d)$ throughout the deployment range. Therefore, expected utility is

$$EU = (1 - p)\, U(m, 1, 0) + p \int_{\mu - \delta}^{\mu + \delta} \frac{1}{2\,\delta} U(m + wd, 1 - d, d)\,\mathrm{d}d \qquad (2.1)$$

An increase in δ increases the variance of deployment time. To isolate the effect of an increase in variance from that of an increase in the mean, let us assume that d_2 increases and that d_1 decreases by the same amount, which increases δ but leaves mean deployment time unaffected. To isolate the effect of increasing the mean, let us assume that d_1 and d_2 increase by the same amount, which increases the mean but keeps the difference $d_2 - d_1 = 2\delta$ constant, and so the variance stays the same.

Expected Utility and Preferred Deployment

If the individual could choose, he or she would maximize expected utility by finding optimal values for p, μ, and δ. These preferred values are written p^*, μ^*, and δ^*. The perspective in this case has the individual looking ahead to the future and, in effect, choosing among distributions of deployment. The individual weighs the expected utility from a high or low probability of the occurrence of deployment, a long or short average length of deployment, and a large or small variance in length. The derivatives of expected utility with respect to p, μ, and δ are as follows:

---

[1] Hosek and Totten (2002) present a Bayesian model of learning in which the individual updates expected utility based on deployment experience. They also consider multiple episodes of deployment.

$$EU_p = \int_{\mu-\delta}^{\mu+\delta} \frac{1}{2\delta} U(m+w\,d, 1-d, d)\,\delta d - U(m,1,0)$$

$$EU_\mu = \frac{p}{2\delta}(U(m+w(\mu+\delta), 1-(\mu+\delta), \mu+\delta) - U(m+w(\mu-\delta), 1-(\mu-\delta), \mu-\delta))$$

$$EU_\delta = \frac{p}{2\delta}(-\int_{\mu-\delta}^{\mu+\delta} \frac{1}{2\delta} U(m+w\,d, 1-d, d)\,\delta d +$$

$$U(m+w(\mu+\delta), 1-(\mu+\delta), \mu+\delta) + U(m+w(\mu-\delta), 1-(\mu-\delta), \mu-\delta))$$

(2.2)

The derivative of expected utility with respect to p equals expected utility given deployment minus utility given no deployment. Interestingly, the derivative does not depend on p, so p is not explicitly or implicitly defined by the derivative. Instead, the optimal value p^* must be inferred by logic. If the derivative is positive, expected utility given deployment exceeds utility without deployment, so some deployment is preferred to no deployment, implying $p^* = 1$. Similarly, if the derivative is negative, then no deployment is preferred to some deployment, so $p^* = 0$.[2] Because preferences differ, some individuals prefer deployment ($p^* = 1$) while others prefer none ($p^* = 0$), and others might be indifferent. Although individuals cannot control whether they deploy, they can satisfy their preferences to some extent when joining the military by choosing the branch and occupational area closest to their preferences.

The derivative of expected utility with respect to mean deployment time μ depends on utility at the longest deployment time minus utility at the shortest deployment time. The optimal value of μ occurs where these utilities are equal; the derivative is zero at that point (assuming it is attainable). With diminishing marginal utility[3] of both home time and time deployed, it is reasonable for utility to increase with deployment time and then to decrease. For instance, at low time deployed, the marginal utility of deployment time is high and the marginal utility of home time is low, so utility increases as deployment time increases. But with high time deployed, the marginal utility of deployment time is low and the marginal utility of home time is high, so utility decreases as deployment time increases. At some point in between, expected utility reaches a maximum ($0 \le \mu^* \le 1$). However, depending on preferences, utility could increase monotonically with deployment time, in which case the derivative is always positive and

---

[2] If expected utility when deployed always equals utility when not deployed, the individual is indifferent and p^* is indeterminate ($0 \le p^* \le 1$).

[3] *Marginal utility* is the incremental increase in utility resulting from a unit increase in one of the arguments of the utility function, holding the others constant. *Diminishing marginal utility* means that the marginal increase in utility becomes smaller at successively higher values of the argument. For example, the first lick of an ice cream cone increases utility by more than the tenth lick.

$\mu^* = 1$. Similarly, utility could decrease monotonically with deployment time, so the highest utility is reached at a mean deployment length of zero and $\mu^* = 0$.[4]

The third derivative shows the effect of an increase in the variance of time deployed. If utility is concave with respect to deployment time, then the individual is risk-averse to variation in deployment time and an increase in variance reduces expected utility. Under concavity, the preferred variance of deployment time is zero ($\delta^* = 0$). Furthermore, if utility is maximized at no deployment ($\mu^* = 0$) or full deployment ($\mu^* = 1$), then any variance in deployment time moves the individual to a lower level of expected utility. Concavity is consistent with our argument above that, at low levels of deployment time, an increase in deployment time increases utility, while at high levels of deployment time an increase in deployment time decreases utility. Again, the optimal variance is zero. Further, even if an exact length cannot credibly be given, the model implies that the individual would prefer to have information that reduced the variance—for example, to know that the deployment will be, say, 12 months long plus or minus a month, rather than a random length centered at 12 months plus or minus two months.

Summarizing, we can see that because preferences differ, some individuals prefer to be deployed ($p^* = 1$) and other prefer not to be deployed ($p^* = 0$). Because the military is an all-volunteer force, it is reasonable to expect that most members prefer some deployment to none. For those preferring deployment, probably most prefer to be deployed part of the period ($0 < \mu^* < 1$), although a few might prefer to be deployed throughout the period ($\mu^* = 1$). Assuming that utility is concave in deployment time (risk-aversion), the optimal variance in time deployed is zero.

Implications

The above analysis suggests a number of key points that recognize that the individual is not free to choose the parameters of deployment and, as a result, the actual values may not equal the preferred values:

- Because the optimal variance of time deployed is zero, the larger the variance is, the lower is expected utility.
- If the member prefers to have some deployment ($p^* = 1$), but deployment is not guaranteed ($0 \leq p^* < 1$), expected utility is reduced. A similar result holds if the member prefers no deployment and that is not guaranteed.
- Any difference between preferred mean deployment time and expected deployment time—i.e., between μ^* and μ—reduces utility.
- A change in p or μ increases or decreases utility, depending on their initial value relative to the preferred value. For some members, an increase in μ increases expected utility because μ moves closer to μ^*, while for others the same change is a movement away from μ^* and reduces expected utility.
- The typical member probably prefers some deployment for part of the period ($p^* = 1$, $0 < \mu^* < 1$). If so, then as μ increases beyond the median value of μ^*, utility

---

[4] In the latter case, the preferred probability of deployment is also zero. This is because expected utility given deployment is less than utility not deployed, so the first derivative above is negative. Similarly, when $\mu^* = 1$ we also have $p^* = 1$.

will decrease for more and more members. The decrease could be more rapid for worse conditions of deployment—for instance, hostile, arduous. For example, if the distribution of μ^* among individuals centers at 0.25 (deployed one-fourth of the time), an increase in μ from this level increasingly tends to reduce members' expected utility. Higher pay could be used to compensate for this decrease. In particular, the deployment pay rate could be constructed to increase as the amount of deployment time becomes greater.

- A large increase in μ would reduce some members' expected utility below expected utility at their best alternative, and they would want to leave the military.
- The military could respond by increasing base pay, deployment pay, or factors affecting the marginal utility of time deployed and home time. Factors affecting the marginal utility of time deployed include, for instance, deployment training, the quality of unit leadership, unit cohesion, living conditions, food, facilities to communicate back home, and provision of supplies and equipment (e.g., body armor). Factors affecting the marginal utility of home time include the quality of housing, schools, health care, family support, recreational facilities, day care, and spouse's employment opportunities (Huffman et al., 2001a).
- The marginal utility of home time and deployed time can depend on the conditions of work. Intensive work—for example, frequently working unusually long duty-days, can be expected to decrease the marginal utility of time spent in military activities and reduce the intention to stay in the military.
- Expected utility is independent of a specific realization of deployment d. That is, the derivative of expected utility with respect to d is zero. Therefore, the current realization of deployment has no effect on expected utility. Although some members may be highly satisfied or dissatisfied with their current deployment and quite vocal in saying so, this current state may have no effect on expected future utility and, hence, no effect on retention.
- However, if the current realization of deployment causes the individual to revise the estimates of p, μ, or δ, or the factors mentioned above, that could affect expected utility. For instance, expectations about the frequency and duration of deployment may have changed markedly because of the operations in Iraq and Afghanistan, which, in turn, might require a change in compensation policy, the management of deployments (e.g., realigning units to broaden the rotation base in order to reduce the frequency or duration of deployment), or an increase in force size.
- Actual deployment might also cause a revision in preferences. For instance, the accumulation of deployment experience could make additional deployment more, or less, satisfying. A specific example of what makes deployment less satisfying is post-traumatic stress disorder, which is especially relevant to first-term enlisted personnel and junior officers who, as civilians, never experienced deployment and who have naïve estimates of p, μ, and δ, and the marginal utility of deployment time and home time. Another example is the toll taken by multiple combat deployments (Zaroya, 2005).

Illustrative Examples

To illustrate the model, we consider three types of individuals.[5] Figure 2.1 shows the relationship between expected utility and mean deployment time for each type. Type 1 prefers to be deployed one-fourth of the time ($p^* = 1$, $\mu^* = 0.25$), type 2 prefers to be deployed all the time ($p^* = 1$, $\mu^* = 1$) and type 3 prefers not to be deployed at all ($p^* = 0$, $\mu^* = 0$).

Type 1 is probably the most common. Personnel in combat and combat support specialties seem likely to prefer some deployment, although not for the entire period. In the figure, expected utility is highest for type 1 at a mean deployment time of 0.25—that is, when, on average, deployment is for one-fourth of the period. Therefore, the preferred level of deployment is 0.25 for our illustrative type 1. Personnel in other occupational areas are likely to have a mixture of preferences for deployment, with many preferring some deployment (type 1) but perhaps a lower average amount of deployment, say, 0.20 or 0.15 in the context of our illustration, and their expected utility would be highest at those levels. Others may prefer no deployment, and their expected utility would be highest at a mean of zero (type 3). A few personnel might prefer deployment all the time (type 2), and their expected utility would be highest at a mean deployment time of one.

In the 1990s, 35 to 40 percent of Army and Air Force personnel had some deployment in a three-year period, compared with 65 to 70 percent of Navy and Marine Corps personnel (Hosek and Totten, 2002). It is consistent with the model

Figure 2.1
Illustrative Preferences for Deployment

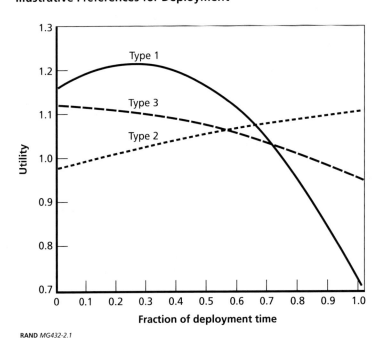

RAND *MG432-2.1*

---

[5] See Appendix A for details.

that some of the nondeployed personnel would have preferred to be deployed, so the actual percentages should not be taken as an indication of preferences. The fact that reenlistment was typically higher for those with one deployment versus those with no deployment suggests that some who were not deployed would have preferred to be. The percentages and average time deployed differed somewhat by occupational area, although the differences were not huge. The similarity in deployment percentages was driven by the fact that units deploy, and units consist of personnel from many occupations. The percentage and average time deployed are undoubtedly higher today than in the 1990s.

Empirical Studies of Retention

As the model implies, increased deployment time is not unambiguously associated with lower utility or lower reenlistment. In fact, there is a considerable body of literature that documents ways deployments can increase utility and have a positive effect on reenlistment. For example, Huffman, Adler, and Castro (2000) found that soldiers on deployment feel more focused on their mission and sometimes experience a reduction in stress because of the elimination of non–job related duties. Huffman et al. (2001a) find that when a deployment includes challenges, chances to use relevant skills, leadership opportunities, and other professional opportunities, personnel are more likely to report that deployment had a positive effect on their decision to stay in the military. Adler et al. (2000) find that personnel who contributed to distributing aid and rebuilding communities in Kosovo were more likely to report increased job satisfaction than were nondeployed personnel.

Several studies support the argument that individuals may experience increases in utility and, as a result, in reenlistment intentions, because of their experiences on deployment. As mentioned, Hosek and Totten (2002) find that reenlistment is higher for personnel with some deployment than for personnel with no deployment. The authors suggest that individuals learn about the satisfactions and dissatisfactions of deployments from being deployed and upwardly update their expected utility from deployment. In the 1990s, the update apparently tended to increase expected utility and the likelihood of reenlisting.[6] Hosek and Totten also find that reenlistment appears to be unrelated to months of nonhostile deployment but appears to decrease with months of hostile deployment—a finding that suggests that different types of deployment may have different effects on individual utility and reenlistment intentions. Hosek (2004) notes that once individuals reach three or more deployments (a combination of hostile and non-hostile), reenlistment probabilities appear to drop somewhat—a finding that is consistent with the model: Utility will decline when the amount of deployment exceeds the preferred amount of deployment.

Fricker (2002) finds similar results for officers: a positive association between nonhostile deployments and continuation of service for junior and mid-grade officers. Hostile deployment has a weaker positive effect for junior officers than does nonhostile deployment, but, in most cases, continuation rates for hostile deployers are still higher

---

[6] Recall that the model implied that a particular deployment realization has no effect on expected utility, unless it causes the individual to update the parameters of the model. For this reason, Hosek and Totten emphasize the learning/updating process.

than for officers with no deployment. For mid-grade officers, hostile deployments are associated with a higher likelihood of continuation, a difference at least partly due to self-selection. Officers who remain in the service longer are also likely to have a better-developed taste for military service and deployment. When deployment length is considered instead of frequency of deployments, the same general relationship holds. Chow and Polich (1980) find that being assigned a specialty that requires spending 25 percent of time away from one's family does not have a negative effect on reenlistment. Adlerks (1992) finds that one-half to one-third of officers and enlisted personnel are satisfied with the amount of time spent away from their families, particularly if total time is less than 27 weeks (half a year). Satisfaction appears to fall somewhat as time away increases above 27 weeks. This finding supports the model discussed above.

Some studies find a negative relationship between deployment and reenlistment, at least for certain types of deployments and certain groups of individuals. Goldberg and Warner (1982) find that the more sea duty a sailor expects in his/her next term, the less likely he/she is to reenlist or extend his/her current term. Golding et al. (2001) found that specific types of deployments and the individual's actual experience at sea can have a negative effect on reenlistment intentions, findings that are consistent with the model discussed above. Deployment factors that might cause the individual to lower his/her expected utility of deployment could have a negative effect on reenlistment. Golding et al. (2001) found that Navy personnel who have been deployed are more likely to leave the service than those who have not. Also, nondeployed time under way is associated with higher rates of attrition for Navy personnel: for every 10-percent increase in nondeployed time away, the authors estimate an increase in attrition of 0.9 percentage points.

The quality of seagoing experience, as measured by number and location of port calls, also appears important to attrition rates. Increased time in "bad ports"—specifically, ports in the Persian Gulf, where there is little liberty, also appears to increase attrition rates. Wong, Bliese, and Halverson (1995) found that previously deployed soldiers are more likely to leave the military, but they found no link between deployments and the psychological well-being or morale of individual service members.

A negative aspect of deployment is the amount of time the member is separated from his or her family. Boesel and Johnson (1984) found that issues related to family separation are among the top reasons for leaving the Navy among members intending to leave. Adler and Castro (2001) found that members deployed on peacekeeping operations cite family separation during and immediately preceding deployment as the most difficult and stressful aspect of deployments and the one with the largest negative effect on their morale. Consistent with the model above, some aspects of deployment may decrease individual utility, in some cases enough to induce separation.

As discussed, deployment pay and other types of special or incentive pays can increase the expected utility of deployments. The literature suggests that effectively compensating individuals for deployment can offset negative effects of deployment on reenlistment. For example, a study of active and Reserve soldiers who volunteered for peacekeeping missions in the Sinai in the 1990s found that soldiers on average had a financial gain from deployment and, further, revealed that volunteers were more likely to intend to stay until retirement if they made financial gains during their deployment (Lakhani and Abod, 1997). Golding and Griffis (2003) found that an increase in Sea

Pay in 1981 led to a 58-percent increase in tour extensions in that year. They also found that sailors are willing to extend sea duty by one year for $150 per month and the guarantee of being based at a domestic, rather than a foreign, port (and 30 percent of those surveyed would have extended just for the $150 per month).

Golding and Griffis (2003) estimate that, given the increase in deployment frequency and length, an additional Sea Pay of $220 to $345 per month for sailors who deploy would offset any negative retention effects. They offer two offsets: (1) Instituting Sea Pay Plus, which would double the amount of compensation individuals receive after six months deployed and would target those with three to eight years of service—the ones making the first-term reenlistment decision and for whom monetary incentives are the most effective—who would receive an extra $300 per month. (2) Restructuring High Deployment per Diem, ITEMPO, pay, for sailors away excessively over a two-year period or for more than six months at a time. The pay would start at $100 per month at month 6 and increase to $300 per month as the duration of the deployment increased; it would compensate individuals for cumulative time away with $100 per month for 400 days away, $200 per month for 450 days away, and $300 per month for 500 days away.[7] Griffis, Hattiangadi, and Gregory (2002) consider Sea Pay with respect to the Seabees, a Navy construction unit. The authors argue that the lower Sea Pay offered to Seabees could, in the long run, hurt the quality and number of personnel recruited to the Seabees in relation to other seagoing ratings.

In support of the importance of effectively structured deployment pay, Boesel and Johnson (1984) found that pecuniary variables are the most important determinants of reenlistment. Chow and Polich (1980) found that military compensation has the most significant effect on reenlistment out of 23 explanatory variables. Goldberg has surveyed studies of pay and retention (2001). Those studies that control for individual heterogeneity (i.e., differences among individuals in their unobserved preference for military service) found a first-term elasticity in the range of 1.0 and a second-term elasticity somewhat lower, in the range of 0.5 to 1.0. (Elasticity is higher in studies that do not control for individual heterogeneity.)

Interestingly, seagoing ratings in the Navy have the lowest reenlistment-pay elasticity (Warner and Simon, 1979), suggesting that, for some occupations, pay has a weaker positive effect on utility, possibly because of the higher deployment rates of these occupations and the negative effects on utility that come along with longer, more frequent deployment. Bonuses also have a strong effect on reenlistment. Chow and Polich (1980) estimated that bonuses are about 60 percent as effective as changes in compensation, with an elasticity ranging from 1.6 to 5.9 (Enns, 1977). Hosek and Peterson (1985) found that bonuses—in particular, lump-sum bonuses—can increase reenlistments and induce individuals to sign longer contractual obligations, even in the face of lower civilian unemployment rates. Goldberg (2001, p. 66) states, ". . . as a rough rule of thumb . . . a one-level SRB [selective reenlistment bonus] increase leads to an increase in the reenlistment rate of about 2 percentage points."

---

[7] Currently, High Deployment Pay has been suspended under Secretary of Defense authority. (Suspension probably resulted from the fact that High Deployment Pay would have reduced the services' ability to flexibly deploy personnel needed for OEF/OIF and, at the same time, would have increased the cost of military operations.) Under the National Defense Authorization Act, it is set at $100 per day for every day a member is deployed past 400 days in any 730-day period, or more than 191 days in a 365-day period.

Aside from pay, the literature discusses other variables that may affect the utility from deployment and military service. Some of these are directly addressed in the model discussed above; others are not explicitly discussed but could fairly easily be included in the utility function. For example, spousal support of the military career may affect utility, both directly and through its effect on family adjustment and marital relations. Rosen and Durand (1995) found that spousal support for reenlistment is a significant predictor of retention behavior. Orthner (1980); Mohr, Holzbach, and Morrison (1981); and Bruce and Burch (1989) found similar results for the importance of spousal attitudes to reenlistment behavior. Spousal support and retention attitudes are also directly relevant to military sociology studies on military-family tension and will be discussed further below.

Hosek and Totten (2002) found that individuals with faster promotion time to E-5 are more likely to reenlist. Swift promotion time is likely to increase utility, because it can contribute to expected career-development opportunities.

Uncertainty about deployments may have negative effects on utility and reenlistment. Uncertainty is addressed in the model through the variance: Any increase in variance of deployments is associated with a decrease in utility. Research supports this hypothesis. Boesel and Johnson (1984) found that deployments are more likely to have a negative effect on reenlistment when they are too long, too unpredictable, or poorly planned. Segal et al. (1999) found that individuals who were given little advance notice of their deployment to Korea (and were originally told that they would not have to deploy) expressed low job satisfaction, lower morale, lower family adjustment, and higher likelihood of leaving the service.

Long work hours can also affect reenlistment and utility. Longer work hours and higher work stress are negatively associated with job satisfaction and intention to stay in the military in Johnson (1996). In Huffman et al. (2001a, b), a majority of personnel cite hours worked as a reason to leave the military, regardless of their career intentions. But other studies suggest work hours will have a positive or neutral effect on reenlistment intentions and job satisfaction. Huffman et al. (2001a, b) also found almost no difference in the number of hours worked by those who leave, stay, and are undecided. For noncommissioned officers (NCOs), working fewer days per week was a predictor of intent to leave the military.

Taken together, all of these factors, along with deployment experience and military compensation, determine the total utility the individual derives from military service and factor into the likelihood that the member will reenlist. Our focus groups and data analysis, discussed in Chapters Three and Four, respectively, will be able to offer further insight into some of the factors that may affect individual utility and reenlistment decisions.

Sociology: Attitudes Toward Deployments, Family Stresses, and Retention

While economic utility models and analysis of retention are able to go a long way toward describing individual reenlistment decisions, tastes for the military, and preference for deployments, studies of deployment and military life in sociology offer a rich perspective on attitudes of service members and their families toward military life. Many military sociologists argue that the study of individual retention decisions must include attention not only to economic factors involved in reenlistment (salary, bonuses), but also normative and affective factors—for example, commitment to a set of values or a community (Shields, 1993).[8] In fact, Moore (2002) found that pride in service[9] is the most powerful explanatory variable in her reenlistment model, exceeding even the contribution of satisfaction with pay and benefits to the individual's intention to reenlist.

These findings suggest that any utility model that describes individual retention behavior must also take into account sociological research on topics such as the small-group dynamics of military units, cohesion, combat motivation, organizational commitment, and the military-family tension created by increased deployment schedules. Existing literature on these topics is relevant to this monograph in two primary ways: It adds variables and considerations for inclusion in the utility model outlined above, helping relate the economic and sociological approaches and thereby extending the scope of understanding, and it offers insight into some of the issues and themes that we explored in our focus groups, which are detailed in Chapter Three. The same is true of the research on stress and performance discussed below.

Small-Group Dynamics and Cohesion

In sociological approaches, small-group dynamics and unit cohesion are concepts key to understanding the effects of deployments and combat operations on military personnel. Within the utility model, bonds formed during deployments and lasting friendships could be considered a positive aspect of deployment that contributes to an individual member's overall attitude toward military service. In the military context, *cohesion* has been defined as "the bonding together of members of a unit or organization in such a way as to sustain their will and commitment to each other, their unit, and their mission" (Johns et al., 1984, p. ix). More specifically, sociologists define two types of cohesion: *social cohesion,* which refers to the emotional and friendship bonds formed within a group, and *task cohesion,* which is defined by a shared commitment among members to a collective goal (MacCoun, 1993).

Several factors contribute to strong group cohesion. For example, propinquity (spatial and temporal proximity) and group membership can lead individuals to feel closer to others in the group than to those outside of it (Zajonc, 1968; Brewer, 1979; Gaertner et al., 1993). Strong leadership (Henderson, 1985, 1990), small group size (Hogg, 1992; Mullen and Cooper, 1993), experience of success (Lott and Lott, 1965), and shared threat (Johnson et al., 1981; Johnson, Johnson, and Maruyama, 1984) may also contribute to strong group cohesion. On the other hand, group turnover and turbulence may weaken cohesion (Henderson, 1985, 1990).[10]

---

[8] Economic, sociologic, and psychological models all allow for monetary and nonmonetary factors as influences on behavior.

[9] Because pride in service is a variable that is absent from personnel records, it is the type of variable that in other models is part of unobserved individual heterogeneity of taste for military service.

[10] The studies cited here are only a small fraction of relevant work on this topic. For a more complete listing of previous research, see MacCoun (1993).

Cohesion may affect group performance and morale. Several studies have tried to clarify the nature and direction of the relationship between unit performance and cohesion. Some studies have found a positive relationship between cohesion and performance (Mullen and Cooper, 1993); other studies have found that increased cohesion may hurt performance (Driskell, Hogan, and Salas, 1987; Kahan et al., 1985). Mullen and Cooper (1993) address this duality, arguing that it is task cohesion, not social cohesion, that contributes most strongly to group performance, because task cohesion facilitates group coordination, goal integration, and within-group performance monitoring. Among several reasons for associating social cohesion with poor group performance is that, as Janis (1983) argues, social cohesion may undermine group decisionmaking processes by promoting conformity and "group think," when individuals ignore important cues in making a group decision.

Finally, the direction of the cohesion-performance relationship is not entirely clear. Although a positive relationship between group task cohesion and performance appears to exist, it could be that successful group performance contributes to strong group cohesion just as significantly as cohesion contributes to group performance (Oliver, 1990) and that negative group performance may foster poor cohesion. Most likely, the relationship is a two-way one, with feedback between cohesion and performance. Importantly, as we discuss later in this chapter, group cohesion may also serve to moderate the effects of stress on group performance, helping groups maintain effective levels of performance in the face of external challenges.

Combat Motivation

Combat motivation—what inspires young people to enlist in the military and continue fighting when on deployment—is another area that military sociologists have explored. This line of research addresses some of the intangibles that are not explicit in the above utility model—for example, what drives individual preferences or tastes for the military and what factors determine the utility that service members derive from their deployment experiences. These topics return in the chapter discussing focus group findings.

Nonmonetary motivations for enlisting and remaining in the military are usually placed into three main categories: personal (to get away from home, to travel), patriotic (to serve one's country), and self-advancement (to learn a trade or make a military career). Looking more specifically at combat motivation, Moskos (1970) argues that a soldier's motivation to fight comes from the interaction of individual self-concern, primary group processes (unit cohesion, the solidarity of a small group), and the shared beliefs of soldiers (ideological commitments). To this list, Kellet (1982) adds the perception of an external threat by the soldier to himself or something he values highly (homeland or family). Several studies have supported the argument that an individual's commitment to his unit or work group and his loyalty to his colleagues can provide combat motivation (Henderson, 1985; MacCoun, 1993; Moskos, 1970; Sarkesian, 1980; Shils and Janowitz, 1948). Furthermore, Moskos (1970) found that while overt ideological and patriotic motivations played a relatively small role in the combat motivations of the average soldier in his study, unstated beliefs about the legitimacy of the social system for which he is fighting did contribute to combat motivation, particularly to the extent that these beliefs were shared. Finally, Moskos asserts that "manly honor" and the perception of combat participation as a sign of masculinity and toughness may also contribute to a soldier's combat motivation. It is worth noting that these studies considered mostly Vietnam-era soldiers, almost all of whom were men, and did not look directly at whether similar factors motivate combat participation for women.

Effects of Operations Other Than War on Morale

Military sociology has focused extensively on the personnel impact of operations other than war (known variously as peace making, peacekeeping, peace enforcement, humanitarian missions, stability operations, nation-building, and so on) (Janowitz, 1960; Moskos 1976; Segal and Segal, 1993), a focus that intensified during the 1990s as these types of operations became more frequent. Scholars and policymakers alike were interested in how military personnel would respond to a new pace of deployments, to include types of missions most did not expect when they volunteered for military service. This interest raises questions similar to the one we are asking in our monograph in the context of the wars in Iraq and Afghanistan, one that is directly related to the expected-utility model, and one that will be explored in more detail in our chapter on focus group findings.

In general, sociologists have found commonalities between troops' attitudes across combat and other types of deployments, including similarities in the life course of attitudes before, during, and after a deployment. Herzog (1992) applied the pattern of attitudes that Fussell (1975) noted in British soldiers during World War I, moving through stages of innocence, experience, and reconsideration, to American soldiers serving in Vietnam, with an additional "aftermath" stage added to account for when soldiers are no longer interacting with their war buddies. In research on United Nations peacekeepers in Cyprus in the 1970s, soldiers' attitudes transitioned from naïve idealism, to cynicism, to a pragmatic approach to the task (Moskos 1976). Similarly, attitudes of the first wave of soldiers serving in Somalia in 1993 revealed high expectations formed in the United States (that Americans would be helping people in need), disillusionment once the reality of the situation was confronted (some Somalis were attacking American soldiers), and practical resolution, either to approach the mission as a warrior would (view Somalis as the enemy and fight back) or to adopt a new humanitarian strategy (view some Somalis as the enemy but the majority as needing and accepting U.S. intervention) (Miller and Moskos, 1995).

These studies show continuity across deployments in cycles of attitudes that are typically lower in the middle of deployment, and higher initially and as the mission comes to a close or has already ended. This finding suggests that one explanation for retention rates that are higher than expected based on reported attitudes overseas or in theater is related to the point in time at which personnel are least satisfied. Highly vocal and negative statements mid-deployment about intentions to leave the military may soften or even turn around as the shock of disconnect between expectations and reality is negotiated and troops become proficient and/or successful in their mission, or in the postdeployment phase, when many of the discomforts of deployment are past and many of the benefits are realized.

Research on the effect of operations other than war on troop morale has also explored reactions to taking on tasks the military had not previously defined as part of its mission, had not trained units to perform in, and which were not expected when people joined the military. As operations other than war became more frequent than in the past, some dissatisfaction was found in response to deployment on humanitarian and peacekeeping operations, particularly among combat units that believed their skills were being degraded. But many troops reported satisfaction with "real-world" missions: making a difference in people's lives, the greater responsibility and more-challenging work on these operations, and the financial and career benefits of deployments (Avant and Lebovic, 2000; Halverson and Bliese, 1996; Miller and Moskos, 1995; Miller, 1997). A study of soldiers serving in Haiti in 1994 found that, even among soldiers who did not believe in the value or overall importance of the U.S. mission, there were those who took satisfaction in seeing their efforts make a positive change in their area of operation (Halverson and Bliese, 1996).

Judging from these studies of peacekeeping missions, we might expect that service members in the combat arms serving in nonhostile areas of the country or in noncombat-like missions (e.g., fighter pilots patrolling a no-fly zone) would be less satisfied with their deployment than engineers helping to rebuild a city or protect a base, or medical personnel applying their skills to serious injuries and diseases. Halverson and Bliese (1996) found evidence to support this expectation, noting that personnel in support units reported substantially higher levels of satisfaction with the Haiti operation than did those in combat-arms units.

This research is particularly relevant to our monograph because it deals with issues similar to those faced by personnel in Iraq and Afghanistan. Although both of these deployments require some actual combat operations, they also require stabilization, peacekeeping, and rebuilding activities that, some military personnel may feel, do not utilize their skills or fall outside of their job requirements. Furthermore, the notion of mission support will also be relevant to the discussion of the relationship between stress and performance, below, because support of mission has been linked to organizational commitment, which may help individuals deal with difficult situations and the challenges faced on deployments.

Other research has considered the readiness of military personnel for operations other than war, in terms of their outlook and attitudes toward military responsibilities. Models of peacekeeping and noncombat missions suggest that such operations require a constabulary force that is committed to minimum use of coercion and is made up of individuals with an international loyalty and commitment to multinational institutions (Janowitz, 1960; Moskos, 1976). According to Moskos (1976), this means that to be effective in nontraditional missions, soldiers may need a high degree of both global commitment and patriotism.

However, Segal and Segal (1993) found that soldiers who are socialized to a "warrior ethos," a mentality characterized by aggressiveness, honor, and readiness for battle that is the norm for military personnel, may have difficulty accepting and rationalizing a noncombat role—especially those individuals who self-select into the military based on the compatibility of the warrior role with their own preferences and personality, as suggested by the utility model above. Yet, with the growth in operations other than war, prospective recruits, as well as service members, have probably come to recognize the changed nature of defense: that today's warrior ethos may mix operations other than war with major theater war operations. Franke (1997) found that among West Point cadets, warriorism (the willingness to go into battle) scores increased steadily over the course of the four-year program, whereas patriotism and globalism decreased significantly, findings suggesting that in the 1990s military socialization programs lagged the emergence of operations other than war as bona fide defense activities.

Finally, military sociology studies on operations other than war have also looked at how these types of deployment affect soldiers' morale and reenlistment intentions. Reed and Segal (2000) looked at this relationship using surveys of members of infantry units assigned to hurricane relief efforts in Florida in 1992, then deployed to Somalia in 1992–1993 and Haiti in 1994. Notably, although morale decreased as the number of deployments a soldier participated in increased, intention to reenlist was not significantly affected. This finding echoes some of the research cited above on the relationship between multiple deployments and reenlistment (e.g. Hosek and Totten, 2002)—a finding that may or may not hold for multiple deployments to the Middle East today, for which deployments may be twice as long, more dangerous, and occur in the same country, rather than provide exposure to a new culture or region of the world. Then, again, as described in the discussion of utility, other factors, such as financial gain and direct satisfaction from deployment, may provide enough of a counterweight to a decline in morale that reenlistment intention may be unaffected.

Military-Family Tension

Sociologists have followed another deployment- and retention-related issue: the persistent tension between the military and the family, two "greedy institutions"—i.e., institutions that make heavy demands for the commitment and time of individuals (Segal, 1988). This strand of sociological research parallels economics studies of labor force participation and hours of work, and also connects to psychological studies of stress caused by work-family tensions. The issue is directly relevant to our research, because the current increase in the frequency and length of deployments has substantially increased the time a service member must spend away from his or her family, because of either deployments or long work hours on base.

Originally, the U.S. military recruited from a base of young, single men, and the only form of family support was family quarters for senior officers on the frontier post (Little, 1971). Mass conscription in World War II led to the introduction of family allowances and limited medical care, which were subsequently preserved and expanded as a way to maintain the postwar volunteer force. After the Korean War, the link between the military-family conflict and retention demanded attention when attitude surveys showed that, for officers, "disruption of family life was one of the major deterrents to career service," and for enlisted, "interference of Army routine with family life" was a significant factor influencing separation (Cline et al., 1955, in Little, 1971). As American women's workforce participation rose and the model of the dutiful military wife declined, it became more of a strain on the family for civilian spouses to withstand frequent moves and single parenthood when their military spouses were overseas (Segal, 1988). The greater participation of women in the military accompanied an increase in dual-military-career couples: A strain on couples who do not have complete control over their assignments or the timing of deployments. Finally, military-family tension has been increased by the changing norms that require men to contribute more to their family roles and to assume more domestic responsibilities (Pleck, 1997).

Recent sociological studies have focused on how military-family tension affects the commitment to the military among military members and their spouses. For example, as mentioned above, an extensive body of research, mostly on military wives, shows that a spouse's attitudes toward military life and the military careers of his or her service member spouse were strongly linked to and predictive of the service member's reenlistment or reenlistment intentions in the 1990s (Bourg and Segal, 1999; Lakhani, 1995; Lakhani and Fugita, 1993; Segal and Segal, 1993). Furthermore, research has found that a spouse's perceptions of the degree to which the military is supportive of families affects the spouse's satisfaction with military life, her (these studies looked at military wives only) support for her husband's military career, and her willingness to tolerate deployment separations (Segal and Harris, 1993). Bourg and Segal (1999) found that perceived unit support for family issues has a direct effect on the spouse's commitment to the military, as well as on the soldier's commitment to the military in the case of the Army. They also found that expected Army policy support for family issues also has a direct effect on the soldier's commitment to the military, but not on the spouse's commitment.

Cohesion and integration of the member and his or her spouse within the military community appear to also affect retention. McClure and Broughton (1988) and Burrell, Durand, and Fortado (2003) reported that integration into the military community is significantly correlated with the spouse's retention attitude, as well as that of the military member. This association could occur because families with a stronger attachment to the military are more likely to cultivate community relationships or because more-welcoming communities boost the family's intention to remain in the military. To some extent, then, military policies that enhance family support programs and military community integration can directly affect the degree of military-family tension experienced by service members and their families, as well as how this role conflict affects reenlistment and retention. Considering this research within the utility model discussed previously, spousal attitudes toward military life and the effect of military lifestyle on work-family tension are variables that are likely to factor into the individual's overall assessment of his military commitment and utility.

Conditions in the current conflicts in Iraq and Afghanistan may contribute to different attitudes than in the past among the spouses of service members toward continued military service. For example, deployments now are longer than those in the 1990s, and more returning veterans suffer from physical disabilities, including amputation and traumatic brain injury, and from post-traumatic stress disorder. The significance of family attitudes on retention and the change in the nature of current deployments call for further research if emerging retention patterns are to be understood and predicted.

Research on the effects of deployment on military families has also focused on a significant moderator of family stress that has grown dramatically in the past two decades: the amount and type of communication between family members during deployments. Beginning in the 1980s, warriors and peacekeepers began to have uncontrolled access to their home and family through telephones, with both positive and negative effects on morale (Applewhite and Segal, 1990; Ender, 1995). In the first Gulf War, personnel had potential access to fax, email, videotapes, teleconferences, telephones, letters, and audiotapes. As deployments continued in the 1990s, these pathways for personal communication grew (Schumm et al., 2004). The rise in real-time, two-way communication—the preferred forms of communication for deployed personnel—

has been a positive step toward providing some "family time" in the midst of the combat zone, and has come to be expected by military personnel (Bell et al., 1999; Ender, 1995; Schumm et al., 2004).

Recent studies have suggested that the ability to communicate home is important for deployed service members and can help to offset negative stresses and the challenges of family separation and deployment (Campbell et al., 1998; Halverson, Bliese, Moore, and Castro, 1995). This communication will be discussed in more detail in the focus group chapter.

Conclusions

Although retention has been considered directly and indirectly in sociological research, no unifying theory has been proposed to understand how these factors come together to shape service members' decisions about whether to remain in the military. The utility model described in the preceding section provides one possible framework, but most likely there are others. To apply and build upon military sociology with regard to the current deployments to Iraq and Afghanistan and to subsequent retention patterns, sociologists would likely examine troops' expectations and attitudes toward the mission, satisfaction with the work itself, unit cohesion and morale during the deployment, spousal attitudes, and deployment-related family issues. Our focus group discussions and data analysis will offer some insight into these issues.

Psychology: Stress and Performance

The literature relating stress to performance is relevant to the preceding discussion of the utility model of deployment, because deployment and military-related stressors and mediators will be factored into an individual's experience of military life and the utility he or she receives from deployment. Furthermore, this literature can offer insight into how deployment-related stressors influence the effectiveness of military personnel, their attitudes toward and satisfaction with military service, and how various aspects of military life may affect their willingness to reenlist. Some of the ideas and themes included in this section, such as the role of unit cohesion, the effects of work-family tension, and the challenges of deployment, are also closely related to those outlined above in the discussion of military sociology. The purpose of this extended discussion is to provide some background on how stress affects individual functioning and performance that will assist in the interpretation of our focus group and data analysis findings.

Many stressors are associated with military life, including those related directly to the military culture and organization and those more specific to deployments and combat operations. In the discussion of the economic utility model, the idea of an individual's "taste for the military" was advanced. Individual tastes and preferences will also be important to a discussion of the effects of stress on performance for military personnel. Edwards and Van Harrison (1993) argue that work strain and individual stress can be caused by a poor fit or mismatch between the individual and the organization or environment, which suggests that individuals whose tastes for the military are weaker or those who fit less well into the military culture may experience more job strain and resulting stress, and possibly even weakened job performance, than individuals who are better suited for military life.

In addition to stemming from general environmental factors, stress may also originate from job characteristics. Edwards and Van Harrison (1993) found that, as job complexity or quantitative workload increases, job dissatisfaction and workload dissatisfaction also appear to increase. This finding connects directly to the economic model outlined previously. Job attributes, such as workload increase or additional job complexity, that lead to job dissatisfaction are likely to affect an individual's attitude toward the military and contribute to his or her reenlistment decision. In this sense, job strain and stress are included as factors in the utility model. Importantly, stressors will affect different individuals in different ways. In fact, different people are likely to classify different stimuli or experiences as "stressful." We recognize that individual differences in stress response and stress coping do exist; the model discussed below is offered as a summary of past research trends and findings, with the understanding that stress will affect the performance of different individuals in different ways and that individuals will vary in their response to stress coping techniques.

Deployment Stressors

We are interested in the stressors relating to deployments, including combat operations, peacekeeping, and other nontraditional missions, and family separations. Combat stressors relate to the pressures, obstacles, and challenges that confront a military member during a contingency operation—threat of death or injury to self or colleagues, fatigue, facing enemy fire, uncertainty about the nature of job requirements, sustained operational tempo, pressure to perform, and physical stressors, such as severe climate or lack of rations.[11]

Recent work on the deployments to Afghanistan and Iraq shed more light on some of the challenges and stressors faced by personnel on these types of operations. Helmus and Glenn (2005) note that, according to their interviews of infantry troops deployed to Iraq and Afghanistan, the urban-combat type of warfare exposes troops to additional types of extreme stressors, including close quarters, the existence of an unidentified and constantly changing enemy, high casualty tolls, and unforeseen obstacles. Work by Hoge et al. (2004) also considers deployments in Afghanistan and Iraq and extends the list of stressors faced by personnel in combat zones. For example, in their survey, taken three to four months after personnel returned from their deployments, the authors found that 58 percent of Army personnel deployed to Afghanistan, 89 percent of Army personnel in Iraq, and 95 percent of Marine Corps members in Iraq had been attacked or ambushed during their deployment.[12] Being shot at or receiving small-arms fire was even more common: 66 percent of Army members in Afghanistan, 93 percent of Army personnel in Iraq, and 97 percent of Marines in Iraq reported having this experience.

---

[11] Kellet (1982) provides an extended discussion of combat stressors and conditions.

[12] The survey results come from several different groups of personnel. The Army group deployed to Afghanistan was surveyed in March 2003, three to four months after their return from a six-month deployment to Afghanistan. The Army group deployed to Iraq was surveyed in December 2003, three to four months after their return from an eight-month deployment to Iraq. The survey results of the Marine group deployed to Iraq were obtained in October/November 2003, three to four months after their return from a six-month deployment to Iraq.

Other deployment stressors are associated with peacekeeping operations and can include uncertainty about individual responsibilities, lack of relevant training, uncertainty about dangers from attack (e.g., mortar attack, suicide bomber, roadside bomb), and even boredom. Surveys of personnel deployed on peacekeeping missions in the 1990s, conducted by Walter Reed Institute, show that some of the most significant stressors reported by personnel are being away from home, lack of personal privacy, lack of time off, disruption of educational goals, long work hours, physical conditions, lack of sleep, martial/relationship problems, and uncertain return or departure dates (Campbell et al., 1998; Halverson, Bliese, Moore, and Castro, 1995). Some of these stressors and their effects on personnel were discussed above in the review of work on operations other than war. Although peacekeeping and combat stressors are different and include some distinct elements, there is significant overlap between the two. For example, combat operations can also include stressors stemming from lack of relevant training or from boredom. Furthermore, peacekeeping and combat operations include a range of physical and environmental stressors, including extreme heat, lack of sleep, poor living conditions, and lack of supplies. Deployments may also lead to work-related stress for nondeployed members, in the form of increased work pace or workload.

Finally, all types of deployments involve separation stressors. Deployments force individuals to leave their families and friends for long, often uncertain, periods of time. This class of stressors affects military personnel who are deployed, families left behind, and colleagues who must deal with their emotions about not being deployed and the additional work left by those who were. It includes the worry associated with being forced to leave one's family alone, financial or safety concerns, and the strain placed on a relationship when individuals are separated. Family separation stressors are also related to the military/family tension issues discussed previously, because deployment represents perhaps the most extreme example of this tension: when the military member is forced to be absent from his or her family role for an extended period of time. Our focus group discussions revealed the importance of family separation stressors in the member's overall evaluation of deployment utility and experience.

Stress and Performance: A Model and Discussion

An understanding of how deployment experience and performance are affected by stressors requires a more detailed discussion of the relationship between stress and performance. Selye (1956) defines *stress* as a nonspecific response of the body to any sort of demand made on it. Selye defines this *demand*, which could include a stimulus or an event, as a stressor and notes that a wide variety of stimuli are capable of producing the same internal stress response. Stressors come in several different forms, ranging from extreme temperature, to time pressure, to a physical assault. According to Selye, once the individual has been exposed to the stressor, a physiological stress response will occur. This stress response can be observed through several different measures, including elevated heart rate, dilated pupils, increased blood pressure, and Galvanic Skin Response (which measures changes in the electrical conductivity of the skin when an individual is aroused/stressed). Figure 2.2 represents the stressor-stress relationship:

Figure 2.2
Stressor-Stress Relationship

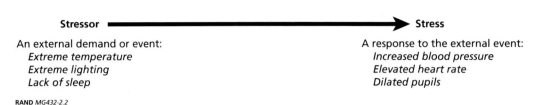

RAND *MG432-2.2*

Effects of Stress on Performance

Stressors and the resulting stress response are likely to affect individual task performance, decisionmaking processes, and perception. This relationship is illustrated in Figure 2.3.

Although the physiological manifestations of stress are largely identical regardless of the form of the external demand, the effects of stress on performance are varied, ranging from physical impairments to cognitive reactions. In general, stress is considered to have a U-shaped relationship with performance, with performance improving as the stressor stimulus reaches a moderate level and decreasing as stimulus strength increases beyond this point (Yerkes and Dodson, 1908; Selye, 1956), although individual differences may exist. In support of this relationship, Srivastava and Krishna (1991) found evidence that an inverted-U relationship exists for job performance in the industrial context.

Critics, however, propose other stress-performance relationship models. Jamal (1985) posited a negative linear relationship, arguing that stress at any level reduces task performance by draining an individual's energy, concentration, and time (see also Vroom, 1964). But optimal performance in Meglino's (1977) model occurs at the highest level of stress, and he argues that, at low levels of stress, challenge is absent and performance is poor (see also Arsenault and Dolan, 1983; and Hatton et al., 1995). Despite some empirical evidence supporting these alternative theories, the inverted-U hypothesis is still the most intuitively appealing and the most used explanation for how stress and performance are related (Muse, Harris, and Feild, 2003).

An extensive body of literature addresses the effects of stress on individual performance and perception. The studies discussed in this chapter represent only a small subset of the studies conducted on the stress-performance relationship and were

Figure 2.3
Stress Can Affect Performance

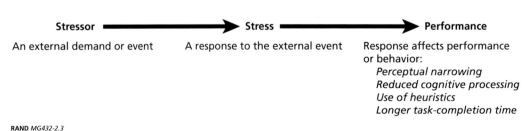

RAND *MG432-2.3*

chosen to be illustrative rather than comprehensive.[13] Many of these studies do not address the military context directly, but their findings should be considered applicable to the performance of military personnel as well. For example, stress can affect an individual's decisionmaking process and ability to make effective judgments. Easterbrook (1959), Janis and Mann (1977), and Friedman (1981) found that when exposed to stressors, individuals experience *perceptual narrowing,* meaning that they pay attention to fewer sensory cues or stimuli that could contribute to their behavior or decision. Peripheral stimuli are likely to be the first to be screened out or ignored. Furthermore, the work of Staw, Sandelands, and Dutton (1981) suggests that individuals may suffer from performance rigidity, or an inability to respond in a flexible and adaptable way, as a result of their reduced search behavior and reliance on fewer perceptual cues to make decisions. Research by Klein (1996) and Shaham, Singer, and Schaeffer (1992) found that, when confronted with external stressors, individuals are more likely to use heuristics (rules of thumb or guidelines based on past experience that are used to help in decisionmaking) and other simplified decisionmaking strategies. Doing so may allow the individual to respond more quickly to an external demand or make an effective judgment with only partial information. However, use of heuristics may also lead to oversimplification of important issues, which can undermine decisionmaking processes. Task-completion time can also be adversely affected by stress. Idzikowski and Baddeley (1983) found that the time to complete a given task doubled with the introduction of an external stressor.

Stress is also likely to interfere with group processes and performance. The previous discussion of small-group dynamics and cohesion indicated that group functioning and processes contribute to personnel motivation and performance. As a result, anything, including stressors that may disrupt these processes or affect cohesion, could have an effect on overall unit morale. Bowers, Weaver, and Morgan (1996) argue that group-level stressors can involve any influence of the group on the individual that leads to increased tension or decreased functioning—for example, competition between members or crowding.

As a result, group decisionmaking processes can be affected by the presence of stressors. Driskell, Carson, and Moskal (1988) found that, when subjected to stressful conditions, individuals are more likely to yield control to their partners or superiors. Authority then tends to become more concentrated and hierarchy more pronounced. Group communication processes are also interrupted and weakened, further impeding effective teamwork, collaboration, and judgment. Stress can lead to what Janis and Mann (1977) call "group think," a process in which members of the group may ignore important cues, force all members to conform or adhere to the consensus opinion, and even rationalize poor decisions.

Maladaptive Stress Reactions

Although the inverted-U hypothesis suggests that exposure to some level of stressor may help individual performance, the majority of research looking at the effects of prolonged exposure to stress has found that long-term effects of stress on the individual tend to be maladaptive, although the ability to handle stress and acceptable stress thresholds may

---

[13] For a more complete discussion of the stress and performance relationship, see Kavanagh (2005).

vary from one person to the next. One potential result of an extended exposure to a single stressor or multiple stressors is *burnout,* defined by Maslach, Schaufeli, and Leiter (2001) as including exhaustion, feelings of cynicism and detachment, a sense of ineffectiveness, and lack of accomplishment. In the extreme, long-term exposure to high levels of stressors or a single exposure to a very demanding event can lead to post-traumatic stress disorder, a psychiatric illness that can interfere with life functioning and that has a variety of symptoms, including nightmares, flashbacks, difficulty sleeping, and social isolation (feeling of aloneness, inability to engage in social interactions).

From the military perspective, the negative effects of long-term exposure to stress are particularly important, because combat and peacekeeping experiences can bring on PTSD or other negative stress reactions, such as extreme anger or mood swings, and depression. In fact, PTSD and its symptoms have been observed in almost all studied veteran populations, including those from World War II, the Korean War, Persian Gulf conflicts, and UN peacekeeping deployments.

In general, the severity of stress response experienced by an individual appears to be related to the type, duration, and magnitude of stressor experienced. For example, Adler and Castro (2001) found that PTSD symptoms are also more prevalent among personnel deployed longer than four months than among those deployed fewer than four months. They also found that soldiers who experience higher levels of peacekeeping incidents (handling dead bodies, disarming militants) report more-significant stress reactions and PTSD symptoms. Adler, Vaitkus, and Martin (1996) support these findings, reporting that Operation Desert Storm veterans who had witnessed U.S. casualties exhibited more-severe PTSD symptoms than those who did not.[14]

Studies of those returning from deployment in Iraq and Afghanistan suggest that stress reactions and disorders also affect these populations. Hoge et al. (2004) found that 18 percent of personnel returning from Iraq exhibit PTSD symptoms, as do 11 percent of those returning from Afghanistan (compared with 9 percent for those who have not deployed). These reactions are of concern for military officials and planners, because mental health issues can affect and undermine the long-term readiness of individual soldiers and units, and the conditions can persist into post-service life.

In addition to chronic stress disorders experienced by returning deployers, military personnel are at risk for other types of stress reactions—for example, Combat Stress Reaction (CSR). CSR usually occurs more immediately than PTSD, while the soldier is still deployed or in the field. It is defined as any stress reaction that renders the soldier ineffective in his or her combat position. Symptoms vary significantly, depending on the battle, the individual, and even social norms, and include fatigue, loss of appetite, anxiety, depression, tremors, or sensory loss. Individuals may be at higher risk for CSR if they have preexisting civilian stressors, low unit cohesion, low self-confidence, low confidence in their commanders, or if they are exposed to prolonged combat, air artillery attacks, surprise attacks, or food/water/sleep deprivation (Helmus and Glenn, 2005).

---

[14] See also McCarroll, Ursano, and Fullerton (1993).

Moderators

Moderators, or intervening variables, affect the relationship between the independent and dependent variables.[15] Within the utility framework described above, moderators are useful because they can help to limit the individual's experience of stress and job strain and the effects that these variables have on overall satisfaction with military life. Several moderators were discussed in the review of literature on military-family tension—for instance, the role of communication with family for soldiers on deployments and the role of perceived unit support for families on spousal attitudes toward the service member's military career. Figure 2.4 shows the two points at which moderators might be able to affect the relationships between stressor and stress response, and stress response and performance.

Although this framework divides moderators into two types, some moderators may function as both type 1 and type 2, depending on the context. For example, as shown in the figure, training can help to reduce the physiological stress response to an external stressor and to prevent performance degradation in the face of stress. The classification of moderators here is based on what appears to be the most common manifestation of the moderator in the literature surveyed.

Type 1 moderators affect the magnitude of the stress response experienced by the individual following exposure to a stressor stimulus. Personality is a significant moderator and can affect an individual's response to stress in several ways. Individuals

Figure 2.4
Moderators in Stressor-Stress-Performance Relationship

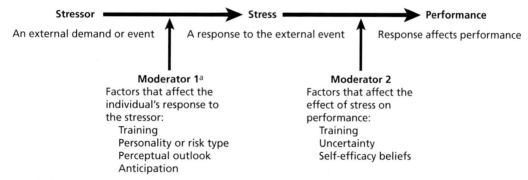

aFor clarity, a moderator at this point will be called "type 1" and a moderator at the second point will be called "type 2."

RAND *MG432-2.4*

---

[15] It is important to distinguish a moderator from a mediator variable. A *mediator variable* intervenes in the relationship between two other variables, is correlated with the first, and has an effect on the second, even when the first is held constant. For example, if *A* mediates the relationship between *X* and *Y* (and *X* and *Y* are correlated), then *X* will be correlated with *A* and it will have an effect on *Y* independent of *X*. A moderator variable affects (usually reduces) the causal relationship between two variables but is not correlated with either variable. For example, if *A* is a moderator for *X* and *Y,* then *A* will reduce the causal effect of *X* on *Y,* but it will not be correlated with either *X* or *Y.* See Barron and Kenny (1986) and Judd and Kenny (1981) for more details.

who express higher levels of anxiety, classified as "high reactivity," have been shown to exhibit more-pronounced physical responses (in terms of heart rate) to stressors (Pearson and Thackray, 1970). Individual perceptual outlook, or attitude toward the world, may also affect the stress response. Lazarus and Folkman (1984) argue that both an individual's experience of stress and stress response are the result of the individual's interaction with the environment and interpretation of the event, based partly on learning and experience.

In the military context, research has defined additional individual characteristics that intervene in the stressor–stress response relationship, including low military rank, socioeconomic status, and minority group membership (Green et al., 1990; Kahana, Harel, and Kahana 1988; Adler, Vaitkus, and Martin, 1996). Importantly, in the military context, some type 1 moderators can be targeted directly at the physical conditions of personnel. For example, Wright, Marlowe, and Gifford (1996) found that showers, mail, tents, and cold drinks were all cited as amenities that helped soldiers deal with the stressors associated with deployment.

Type 2 moderators intervene in the stress response–performance relationship. A helpful moderator allows the individual to maintain a high level of performance despite the existence of arousal or physical response to an external stressor. Jex and Bliese (1999) determined that self-efficacy beliefs (beliefs in one's own ability or competence to complete a certain task) moderate the negative effects of high work overload and long work hours on an individual's self-reported stress levels. Glass and Singer (1972) found that additional information can reduce the influence of stress on performance by giving individuals a better base for their decisions and improving the accuracy of their expectations. Work by Wright, Marlowe, and Gifford (1996) confirms the moderating effect of additional information for deployed personnel.

Uncertainty or lack of control can be considered a negative moderator, one that magnifies the effects of stress on performance. According to Leitch (2003), uncertainty can increase the negative effects of stress on performance in three key ways: (1) by forcing the individual to spend additional time preparing responses for a range of possible outcomes; (2) by contributing to delay in action and even additional physiological response to stress as the body is forced to "stand by"; and (3) by leading to disaster or worst-case scenario thinking that can distract the individual from the task at hand. Uncertainty was also highlighted in the economic-utility model, in the form of variance of deployment. Extending the findings on uncertainty's role in the stress-performance relationship to the notion of utility suggests that additional variance or uncertainty of deployment could increase individual stress and potentially have a negative effect on utility. This hypothesis is supported by the model discussed above and will be tested in our data analysis in Chapter Four.

In the military context, training—specifically stress-exposure training—is one of the most important moderators, not only because it is extremely effective for many individuals but also because military planners and officials can easily manipulate it. Stress-exposure training allows individuals to practice performing complex tasks while being confronted with an external stressor. This training fosters task mastery and allows individuals to build strategies to counteract stress and maintain performance under difficult conditions.

Many studies offer empirical evidence of the positive effect (reduction) of training programs on individual performance decrement under stress.[16] For example, Hytten, Jensen, and Skauli (1990) found that offshore oil workers who underwent stress-exposure training performed better when undertaking a work-related training task and required less help from the instructors. Sheehy and Horan (2004) found that first-year law students who went through stress-exposure training experienced significant reductions in their reported anxiety and stress levels. Furthermore, those students who received the training and were expected to finish in the lower 20 percent of their class using their Law School Aptitude Test (LSAT) scores as a predictor, displayed significant academic improvement. Using meta-analysis, Saunders et al. (1996) determined that training has consistently been shown to improve performance and reduce individual anxiety in a given situation. Within their sample, stress-exposure training has a moderate, statistically significant effect on improving performance.

In the military context, Helmus and Glenn (2005) found that combat service, combat service support personnel, and Reserve units that come under fire are much more susceptible to severe stress reactions than are special operations or infantry troops. One possible explanation is that the stress-exposure training given to infantry personnel, which includes dealing with dead noncombatants, unconventional combatants (women and children), lifelike injuries, surprise attacks, and live-fire actions, can help prevent high CSR rates among deployed personnel by preparing them in advance for situations they may face in urban combat.

Moderators can also affect group performance under stress, particularly within the military context. Leadership can significantly reduce the negative effects of stress on group performance. Kirmeyer and Dougherty (1988), for example, found that a leader's characteristics, including effective communication and motivational skills, can limit the influence of stress on team performance and contribute to unit morale and efficiency. Unit cohesion, discussed above, was also found to be an important group-level moderator of stress. Milgram, Orenstein, and Zafrir (1989, p. 186) suggest that "a cohesive group may be regarded as an optimal support system in a time of crisis because it provides emotional support, information, instrumental help, and companionship." Helmus and Glenn (2005), in their work on stress reactions during urban combat operations, found that units with high cohesion rates, good leadership, and high morale were less likely to lose personnel for reasons related to job stressors. Griffith (1998) also supports the relevance of unit cohesion as a moderator, finding that units with higher cohesion are also likely to have increased reciprocal learning, higher personal morale, and lower levels of overall reported stress.

Finally, as for individuals, training and stress-exposure training can help to improve group performance. Kozlowski (1998) found that simulated training that mimics the work environment is effective in moderating the effect of the stress response on group decisionmaking processes. Johnston, Poirier, and Jentsch (1998) found that teams that have practiced together are better able to maintain performance levels under

---

[16] The studies on the effects of training discussed here are representative of a much larger body of work on this topic, too numerous to cite here. For further information, see, for example, Adams (1981), Altmaier and Happ (1985), Deffenbacher and Hahnloser (1981), Finger and Galassi (1977), Mace and Carroll (1985), and Sweeney and Horan (1982). Also, Saunders et al. (1996), described in this document, provides a good list of relevant studies.

conditions of external stress. Serfaty, Entin, and Johnston (1998) looked at a specific type of training, known as team adaptation and coordination training (TACT) and found that the groups that received TACT performed significantly better than those in the control group and exhibited a higher teamwork score (a measure of team orientation, communication behavior, monitoring, feedback, and communication content).

Conclusion

This discussion of the relationship between stress and performance offers some insight into how deployment and work-related stressors affect individual and group task completion and functioning. The findings outlined above inform the utility model discussed at the beginning of the chapter by defining additional variables that may affect service members' attitudes toward deployments, and they offer a somewhat different perspective on some of the military sociology issues outlined above—specifically, group cohesion and the potential effects of deployment conditions on individual service members and units.

Summary

The disciplines of economics, sociology, and psychology all contribute useful ideas to the question of how deployments affect military members and their families. In addition, each discipline has a body of empirical work to substantiate the insights from the conceptual approaches of the discipline. The economic model presented here emphasizes the underlying role of individual preferences for deployment and for nondeployment, and the fact that the individual's choice of service and occupation are ex ante choices—i.e., made before the actual realization of deployment outcomes. Depending on individual tastes, a person might prefer a high or a low level of deployment, and the person will choose the service and occupational area that best accords with his or her preferences. Having made that choice, the individual, now a military member, will be deployed according to service needs: Most service members have little control over where, when, and how they will be deployed but, rather, are deployed with their unit as it is needed for defense operations. The actual amount and conditions of deployment might be less, or more, than the individual preferred, and less or more than the individual expected. If actual deployment does not equal expected deployment, the individual might have a lower or higher level of satisfaction than expected. However, if deployment is, for example, far greater than expected, the level of satisfaction is likely to be lower than expected and perhaps lower than preferred. In addition, the member might change his or her expectation of future deployment. For example, extensive current deployment, along with the prospect of a high rate of deployment in the future, would lead to an increase in future expectations of deployment, and this increase would affect the member's expected utility of remaining in the military.

The economic model of deployment assumes that the member has preferences over both time not deployed and time deployed. Just as deployment can have satisfying as well as burdensome aspects, time not deployed will have good and bad points, too. A high pace of deployment operations will require an intensive effort by the nondeployed to make sure that deployed forces are well supplied; that units readying to deploy will have the equipment, training, health care, and administrative support necessary; and that units returning from deployment are squared away (for instance, their equipment has been accounted for, cleaned, serviced, and repaired; action reports have been submitted; personnel records have been updated; family-reintegration counseling has been provided as needed; personnel have been screened for PTSD) and given the support needed to regenerate. Further, satisfaction from deployment can be affected by policy. The economic model allows for both monetary and nonmonetary factors. However, whereas it is explicit in identifying base pay, deployment pay, home time, and deployment time, it is not explicit about other factors.

Although we use an economic model as a point of departure for this chapter, literature from military sociology and psychology make equally important contributions to understanding how deployments and the demands of military life affect individual service members, unit functioning, and the lives of military families. As discussed, sociology has, in particular, been concerned with individual attitudes, group behavior, and organizational culture and structure. Studies of small-group dynamics have highlighted the relationship between unit cohesion and group performance, as well as the role of bonding as a source of motivation to act when in combat. Studies of combat motivation have highlighted shared ideological concerns and perceived threat. Attitudinal studies traced the change in attitudes over the course of a deployment to Cyprus or Somalia from naïve, to cynical, to pragmatic. In these deployments, attitudes tended to be lower in the midst of deployment than at the beginning or the end, which caused some military leaders to speculate during the deployment that postdeployment retention would be low, when, in fact, it turned out not to be. Although peacekeeping involved activities that troops had not been trained to do and did not expect to do, many troops found the activities to be a satisfying achievement—a chance to make a real contribution. Sociology also has recognized the stress that military service, with its seemingly insatiable demand for the member's time, can place on family relationships. Military families with working spouses are tugged in two directions, and this tension may change when the member goes on a long deployment. Sociologists have emphasized the importance of family support and family reunification programs. Our research was able to add to the ongoing debate surrounding some of these issues through our focus groups and survey analysis, discussed in the following chapters.

Turning to psychology, studies of stress have clarified the roles of stressors, stress, and stress moderators. In the context of deployment, these elements encompass stress from combat; moderators that affect the response to a stressor, such as training, and anticipations and perceptual outlook; and moderators that can alter how stress affects performance, such as training, self-efficacy, and uncertainty. Psychology research has also helped in developing training programs that enable individuals and groups to perform more effectively under stressful conditions and deal more effectively with work-related challenges. When combined, the psychology and sociology literatures help to explain how family-support programs, communication links to home, counseling, and chaplains are important to a member's well-being, and why training, equipment, leadership, and medical care can moderate stress by contributing to the member's assurance of being well prepared for deployment missions.

All three perspectives suggest that, as deployments become increasingly frequent and lengthy, deployments will have a more pronounced effect on service members. The economic model implies that, as members are asked to deploy more often and for longer periods of time, increasingly many members will have more deployment than they expected and more than they preferred, which will lead to a decrease in their expected utility from continuing in military service. The sociological literature has focused on how increased demands by the military cause tension between work and family life and on the roles of unit cohesion, leadership, and combat motivation. It has also revealed that deployments affect morale. Finally, the psychological literature on stress and performance suggests that prolonged exposure to the stress associated with combat and peacekeeping operations, particularly if there is a lack of appropriate training, can lead to reduced individual and group performance and contribute to adverse mental health reactions.

Each strand of literature highlights aspects of behavior affected by deployments, and these aspects deserve attention when considering the effects of increased deployment length and frequency on military service members. Steps to spread deployment over more troops, to keep deployment duration within "reasonable" bounds, to increase relevant training, to provide communication and support to families, to reduce uncertainty about the beginning and end dates of deployment, and to increase the flexibility of deployment pay, allowing pay rates to depend on such factors as duration, danger, and difficulty (arduousness), will help to counteract adverse effects generated by an intensive schedule of deployments.

CHAPTER THREE

Focus Group Findings: Stresses and Benefits of Deployments

One of the most intriguing contradictions between the attitudes of military personnel during deployment and their behavior afterward is that, despite complaints registered in-country, deployed troops have been found to be more likely to reenlist than have their nondeployed peers (Hosek and Totten, 2002). Reports from commanders in the field and studies based on interviews with deployed personnel have documented negative attitudes toward serving in overseas operations, particularly due to separation from family, harsh living conditions, and an unknown return date. During the 1990s' operations other than war, some troops rejected policing or humanitarian missions as inappropriate for military units, and they questioned the long-term effectiveness of temporary military interventions. Judging from these attitudes, one might conclude that nondeployed troops stationed at home near their families, living and working with modern Western conveniences, and undertaking typical military missions would have been more likely to reenlist than their deployed counterparts. Not so: Soldiers who deployed in the 1990s tended to have higher reenlistment rates than those who did not. This finding suggests that either certain deployments have positive aspects that contribute to higher reenlistment rates among deployed personnel or that nondeployed military life has aspects that contribute to lower retention among personnel who do not deploy. Some combination of both explanations is also possible. However, it is also important to note that the surprising relationship found between deployment and retention in the 1990s may be limited in its applicability to the attitudes of currently deployed personnel, given the drastically different nature of the missions in Iraq and Afghanistan than that of previous operations.

Statistical analyses have proven the significance of the relationship between deployment and reenlistment rates for earlier deployments; however, survey data have not yet adequately explained that significance. Therefore, we conducted exploratory focus groups with military personnel from each of the services who had and had not been deployed. Our goal was to uncover possible explanations for the correlation between deployment and retention, rooted in the experiences and attitudes of military personnel. Our intention was to identify new perspectives that could be measured in future large-scale random surveys of personnel to determine how representative and how strongly these new elements explain the behavior of the military population at large. Furthermore, we hoped that focus groups with personnel deployed in recent combat operations would offer insights into how, if at all, current deployments and their effects on personnel attitudes differed from those of previous decades.

Our exploratory research was successful in delineating the positive aspects of deployment, especially when evaluated postdeployment, and the negative aspects of garrison life. We also confirmed that previous characterizations of the negative aspects of deployment apply to the current operations in Iraq and Afghanistan.

In the remainder of this chapter, we first outline the methods used in conducting the focus groups, including the types of topics covered and the composition and number of groups. We then turn to a more detailed discussion of the findings from the focus groups—for example, the stressors and benefits of deployment for personnel who deployed, the ways that service members cope with their deployment experiences, and the stressors and experiences of those who did not deploy.

Methods

To solicit the kind of information we expected from the focus groups, we selected military bases with units that had returned from service in Iraq and Afghanistan. To uncover as many different perspectives as possible, we actively sought personnel involved in a range of air, sea, and ground units from a range of occupations. We also wanted to speak with personnel who had not deployed. By contacting Army, Navy, Marine Corps, and Air Force officers, we obtained permission to conduct focus groups at a military installation in each branch of service. Focus group participants included ground troops at Marine Corps Base Camp Pendleton and the Army's Fort Carson, Colorado; sailors at Naval Station Mayport, Florida; and personnel in aviation at Marine Corps Air Station Miramar, California, and Davis-Monthan Air Force Base, Arizona.

We were primarily interested in examining the effect of deployment on enlisted personnel facing either their first- or second-term reenlistment decision. We requested that each of the services provide 80 enlisted personnel in grades E-3 through E-6, to include a mix of recently deployed and not deployed, to fill 10 focus groups of eight people each. We also asked that the services include people from a variety of occupations. After the first set of focus groups, we requested that no one new to the service be included (because they had few experiences thus far to draw upon). Table 3.1 shows the actual number of participants and groups for each service. As the numbers reflect, the turnout from the Army and Marines was below that of the other services, but still sufficient to include troops with some variety of backgrounds and experiences. The lower turnout reflected their intense preoccupation with deployment-related activities.

To supplement our inquiry, we asked for a similar selection of junior officers grades O-1 through O-3 for two focus groups of eight each. Table 3.2 shows the actual participation and number of groups per service. The Army was particularly underrepresented in this category.

Table 3.1
Size of Focus Group for Enlisted (E-3–E-6) Personnel, by Service

Focus group session	Army	Navy	Marine Corps	Air Force
Total participants	53	83	57	80
Number of groups	7	10	10	10
Average group size	7.6	8.3	5.7	8

Table 3.2
Size of Focus Group for Officers (O-1–O-3), by Service

Focus group session	Army	Navy	Marine Corps	Air Force
Total participants	6	15	14	16
Number of groups	2	2	2	2
Average group size	3	7.5	7	8

The focus groups were conducted in the first half of 2004 at each of the sampled military bases, and the sessions lasted between 1.5 and 2 hours, and were typically led by one facilitator assisted by a dedicated notetaker (occasionally the facilitator was also responsible for taking notes, and in a few instances an extra researcher/notetaker was present). Our RAND focus group team had four people. With two people assigned to each focus group, we could hold two focus groups three times a day. The settings included classrooms, offices, and boardrooms that allowed for a secure (i.e., private, interruption-free) environment for the discussions.

The sessions began with a description of the study, including its primary focuses, its sponsors, the researchers' backgrounds, how people were selected to participate, the eventual research product, and its intended audience. Then, focus group members were advised that their participation was voluntary, their responses anonymous, and that the information gleaned would be used solely for this monograph and subsequently destroyed. Participants were given the opportunity to ask further questions about the study, offered contact information for the team, and informed of the Web site on which they would be able to access the monograph once the study was completed. The vast majority of enlisted personnel were in ranks E-3 through E-6, and most officers were in ranks O-2 through O-3.[1]

One of the strengths of a focus group is its ability to generate information unfamiliar to the researchers. Focus group facilitators can introduce a topic and then guide a general discussion among participants, allowing them the flexibility to introduce novel topics and move the conversation into the areas that matter most to them. Members' insider information frequently jogs the memory of other participants, again improving the likelihood that the researchers will discover concepts unknown to them. This semi-structured protocol permits some consistency across groups and encourages a discussion suitable for discovering a wide range of ideas, which was our goal.

To provide some structure to the discussions without unnecessarily limiting them, we developed the topic outline shown in Table 3.3. The topics were intended to encourage members to comment about their expectations, realizations, unexpected challenges, adaptations, stressful experiences, family relations, and intentions to continue in the military. The

---

[1] An O-2 is a First Lieutenant in the Army, Marine Corps, and Air Force, and a Lieutenant, Junior Grade, in the Navy. An O-3 is a Captain in the Army, Marine Corps, and Air Force, and a Lieutenant in the Navy. An O-4 is a Major, except in the Navy, where an O-4 is a Lieutenant Commander. Enlisted ranks are as follows. Army: E-3, Private 1st Class; E-4, Specialist or Corporal; E-5, Sergeant; E-6, Staff Sergeant. Navy: E-3, Seaman; E-4, Petty Officer 3rd Class; E-5, Petty Officer 2nd Class; E-6, Petty Officer First Class. Marine Corps: E-3, Lance Corporal; E-4, Corporal; E-5, Sergeant; E-6, Staff Sergeant. Air Force: E-3, Airman First Class; E-4, Senior Airman or Sergeant; E-5, Staff Sergeant; E-6, Technical Sergeant. Ranks E-1 through E-4 include junior enlisted personnel, and ranks E-5 and above include noncommissioned officers (NCOs).

topic list did not result directly from our literature review; however, we did draw on some of the major themes of existing research—for example, the effect of family separations, the importance of deployment pay, and the stresses of deployments and military life—in the more-specific questions asked during the focus groups.

The content and depth of topic coverage varied from group to group: Most topics were covered in all groups, but some were covered sparsely or not at all, depending on the experiences of the group (i.e., people who had never been deployed could not speak about how deployments compared to their expectations) and the depth or breadth at which other topics were discussed. The focus group environment stimulated individual reminiscence and spontaneous interaction, including movement from one topic to another and back, so that the topics were not necessarily addressed completely (e.g., when a new speaker began on the current topic but his/her comment led to a different topic on which the next speaker commented), or in the order listed in Table 3.3.

Following the focus groups, we transcribed the notes into an electronic file, developed analytic codes, and organized the notes according to our scheme. We used QSR N6 software, a qualitative-coding software product that allows users to organize and systematically analyze qualitative data such as focus group comments. The software allowed us to create a coded, electronic database that enabled us to review, sort, re-sort, and analyze comments in myriad ways. Our goal was to discover as wide a range of explanations as possible for why military personnel who have deployed might be more likely to reenlist than their counterparts who have not deployed.

We now focus on the stresses and benefits of deployment for those deployed, as well as the stresses of deployment on those not deployed. Some themes surfaced more frequently than others; some were felt more deeply than others. We organized the findings this way to illuminate some of the pros and cons of deployment that service members may weigh when considering whether to change jobs, bases, or services; to volunteer for another deployment; or to reenlist for another term. The service members we interviewed revealed explanations for why troops might find deployments fulfilling, despite the stresses on themselves and their families. Service members also explained why those "spared" deployment might be more dissatisfied with military life than their deployed peers.

Table 3.3
Topic List for Focus Group

- Expectations of service life
- Expectations of deployments
- How experiences compared to expectations
- Most valuable experiences from training, schools, and deployments
- Unexpected challenges
- How service members adapt to the unexpected
- Suggestions for improved preparation for service life and for deployments
- Reenlistment, education, and career plans

Deployment Stressors and Deployed Personnel

As Chapter Two indicated, the negative aspects of past deployments are better documented than the positive ones. Our research confirmed the persistence of some of the stressors present in current operations: separation from family and friends, uncertain deployment dates, high work tempo, and austere living conditions. Unlike in the deployments of the 1990s, however, for many personnel deployed recently to hostile zones, coping with the injury or death of colleagues, physical challenges, and exposure to danger were also significant sources of stress. Personnel in our focus groups also pointed out that there is "preparation stress," which occurs in the predeployment phase, and there are reintegration/readjustment stressors that personnel must face postdeployment.

Preparation Stressors

Although *deployment length* usually refers to the period between the time the service member leaves the United States and the time he or she returns, in reality the stressors associated with the deployment begin before the member even departs. The predeployment stressor that we heard about in our focus groups was *preparation stress,* which includes long work hours and frequent training drills or exercises to get the unit ready for deployment, as well as more-personal issues of preparation, such as making financial or other arrangements for the member's absence. On the personal side, many single service members noted that, before deploying, they had to arrange for someone to pay their bills. For married personnel, making sure their family was taken care of was cited as a stressor.

Preparation stress also involved a significant amount of advance work to get the unit ready for deployment. According to service members in our focus groups, in the weeks leading up to deployment, workdays were often extended to accommodate additional training exercises and maintenance jobs that needed to be accomplished before the unit could leave. For example, pilots had to complete the required flight hours to qualify them for service and maintainers needed to prepare tanks and aircraft for deployment. Personnel commented that, although some of this advance work was necessary, the hectic work pace it created increased their stress level and took them away from their families for extended periods of time, even before they left their home base.

Increased work pace also interfered with personal preparations, by making it more difficult for the member to find time to set his/her personal affairs in order:

> There's lots of training, too. For a typical deployment, there are two short exercises and anti-sub training for three weeks. The days you'd want to spend with your family, instead you're supposed to spend at work in 14- to 16-hour days; plus, training exercises take you away from your family before the deployment.

> Doing the deployment is better than working up to the deployment. You might have 10 inspections that are virtually all the same. . . . You should just have one big inspection before deployment to see [that] all the equipment and all the family stuff are squared away.

> In the Navy, you're so busy in the job the last two to three months before you go on deployment you work 7 a.m. to 6 p.m. every day. I was an admin officer and was really involved with everyone. I had to make sure they had their finances in order so they could go to sea without problems.

As the above statements suggest, the preparation stressors that characterize the predeployment phase mean longer hours, less time off, and increased pressure to complete tasks. Personal preparation, including financial matters and family affairs, also make the predeployment phase a stressful one for service members. Because of the demands of preparing for deployment, the predeployment phase basically constitutes an extension of the deployment from the perspective of the service member and his/her family.

Operational Tempo: Longer, More-Frequent Deployments

The effect of increased operational tempo on soldier morale and reenlistment intentions is another important theme that came up throughout our focus group discussions. In general, personnel reported that deployments were becoming longer and more frequent, with less time between deployments. Personnel in all services reported deploying for periods of up to one year and often had only six months at home before deploying again. Deployments were somewhat more predictable for Navy and Air Force personnel, and somewhat shorter for Air Force members. However, focus group participants from all services noted that deployment pace and length had increased since 9/11.

Some focus group members commented that increased operational tempo had a negative effect on their attitudes toward the military and contributed to lower morale and even negative reenlistment intentions:

> A lot of Marines in my squad are getting out. My unit had to do two short-notice deployments—one month['s] notice and seven months deployed, followed by a month at home and seven months in [Operation Iraqi Freedom]. We love deployment, but we're worn ragged.

> An increased operational tempo will have an impact. If the operation in Iraq doesn't wrap up, it will just wear on the deployed unit. Now we have six months deployed and six months off, and this used to be 15 months on and 12 months off.

Although this pace and the time away from home it included were stressful and exhausting for many personnel, others reported that they found the high pace challenging and exciting:

> Tempo is intense. The ones who stay in thrive on this intensity, but many will leave.

Other service members were somewhat less affected and did not think their reenlistment intentions would change as a result of increased operational tempo. Although participants differed on whether or not they thought that the increased pace and length of deployments would have a long-term effect on the willingness of individuals to reenlist, they generally agreed that the current pace of deployments was difficult and exhausting to sustain. These findings accord closely with the model discussed in Chapter Two. Increases in the amount of deployment are likely to affect the overall utility of individual service members in different ways.

As the focus groups reveal, some members do experience decreases in utility as the amount of deployment exceeds their preferred level. For certain individuals, this decrease in utility is enough to cause the member to leave the service, while for others it is not.

Work Pace and Hours During Deployment

Another source of deployment-related stress that was mentioned by most of our focus group members who had deployed was longer work hours and increased work pace while on deployment. Service members across services reported that deployments tended to involve longer work days (often more than 12 hours) and fewer days off. Some personnel commented that, on deployments, they often worked seven days a week for several months and had little time to sleep. Personnel also reported an increased pressure to complete important tasks quickly while on deployment. Interestingly, some service members welcomed the longer working days as a way to keep themselves busy and distracted from homesickness or thoughts of family. In contrast, others felt exhausted or burnt out because they were constantly "at work":

> Deployments have longer hours . . . constant drills, GQs [general quarters], scenarios. Lots of standing watch. And if your watch is at night, you still work days.

> Drivers [in Iraq] had to drive all day and all night because the convoy had to keep moving and there was no one to switch off with.

> We had only five to six hours of downtime per day to do everything—shower, laundry, eat, sleep. We usually got only three to four hours of sleep a night for the first four months there.

> Flight-line operational tempo is really high on deployment. We have a real mission, work 13- to 14-hour days with few days off.

In general, service members recognized that increased work pace and longer work hours were often necessary to complete vital missions on deployment. However, this recognition did not change the fact that the pace of operations and constant grind were exhausting and stressful for deployed personnel.

Physical Challenges and Exposure to Danger

Not surprisingly, many service members with whom we spoke reported that physical and environmental stressors, including extreme temperatures, lack of supplies, and poor living conditions, were significant sources of stress on deployment. Personnel in all services reported that adjusting to new environments and different living conditions on deployments was challenging. For example, Navy personnel found being confined to a ship 24 hours a day, in small berths, difficult at first. For personnel deployed to places such as Iraq and Afghanistan, physical stressors were even more important and made daily life uncomfortable. Personnel reported having to wear full gear in temperatures as high as 120 degrees Fahrenheit, survive with only one meal ready to eat (MRE) per day, and avoid large insects:

> There was no running water. There were land mines. And the bathroom was in a Port-A-Potty. . . . We were attacked, shot at, had to eat MREs, and the water was rationed.

> The only way to describe [living conditions in Iraq] is to imagine putting baby powder in everything, every crack, and [in] food. Then turn the oven on, shut all the windows, and turn on the fan. Then imagine having to deal with jumping bugs, camel spiders, flies . . .

> At first, we lacked the essentials, water and food.

Exposure to danger is another environmental-related stressor that was reported by members in our focus groups, particularly those in the Army and Marines who had been deployed to hostile-fire areas:

> Every time that you are outside the base, even when you are on a forward operations base, you don't feel safe. The threat is constant.

Interestingly, many personnel in our groups tended to agree that this fear of death or attack dissipated somewhat after more time had been spent in the theater. Some personnel with whom we spoke reported that they became somewhat immune to or unaffected by the dangers facing them. For Navy and Air Force personnel, danger on deployments was less of a concern. Personnel in these services noted that they felt pretty safe and out of harm's way:

> It doesn't bother me anymore—if I get shot at, big deal. I don't worry about it.

> I didn't know if I'd get home alive—am I coming back or not? In Iraq, I was shot at almost every day.

> They blew up the side of the USS *Cole* and it didn't sink. I'm not worried.

As the comments above suggest, there are many environmental and physical stressors with which service members are forced to deal while on deployments. Most personnel in our focus groups felt that difficult physical conditions, lack of supplies, and exposure made completing missions and functioning effectively on deployment more challenging. However, most agreed that these types of stressors could be overcome. However, dealing with these types of dangers and hazards may affect the overall utility a member derives from deployment.

Uncertainty

We heard in our focus groups that deployments included uncertainty both before and during the actual deployment. The model in Chapter Two suggested that increased variance and uncertainty about deployment would decrease individual utility. Our focus group discussions confirmed this implication. We heard from discussants that the uncertainty and ambiguity surrounding deployments caused service members considerable concern and made effective performance and job completion more difficult. Return and departure dates, as well as the destination of deployments, were also extremely uncertain and constantly changing. In fact, it was common during our focus groups for members to spend several minutes speculating and disagreeing among themselves about when their unit would next be deployed and to where. Personnel were frustrated at the lack of information provided to them about the timing and nature of deployments.

Even more common was uncertainty surrounding the nature of the unit's mission while on deployment. Personnel were sometimes not told in advance what type of work their unit would be performing or the specific nature of their mission until right before or even on the deployment. Furthermore, focus group members deployed to Iraq reported that, while on deployment, the requirements of their jobs and the tasks assigned to their unit were ambiguous, uncertain, and constantly changing. For example, several service members reported that they were assigned to fill positions in Iraq that did not correspond to their military occupational specialty (MOS) and that they were not trained to complete. Because predeployment training, in some cases, did not address what turned out to be the nature of the Iraq conflict, additional uncertainty existed for members who were unsure of how to act in an unfamiliar situation (hostage taking) or lacked firm knowledge of how to complete their jobs (for example, drive a stick shift). Some personnel in our focus groups also noted that the job of any individual or unit could change from day to day.

Importantly, however, personnel also reported that they were able to adapt and become proficient at the new tasks and demands that deployments presented, even when previously received training did not precisely match the realities of operations. Service members with whom we spoke felt that this ability to adapt quickly to uncertain conditions contributed greatly to their successful mission completion on deployments. Several focus group members agreed that at least some of this uncertainty is unavoidable, because combat situations involve unknown and unexpected contingencies. However, members of our focus groups tended to think that the military needed to do a better job informing service members about the timing and nature of upcoming deployments, when doing so would not jeopardize security, and where possible, providing the appropriate training to allow personnel to perform their jobs effectively:

We were told constantly that we would go home next month, but we never did. This caused morale to drop a little, but you get over it.

When you're deployed, you expect . . . a lot of unknowns, waiting, uncertainty, and lack of consistency in your workday. . . . But we can't prepare because we don't know what's going to happen.

You never know on a ship when, where, or what route you'll go.

In Iraq, we worked at a border crossing. This was not our MOS. We went to Iraq with warfighting skills, but our job there was totally different. By the end, we were proficient.

Our training focused on unit-on-unit combat, not how to handle insurgents. It taught us how to take down an armored vehicle, not how to flush out RPGs [rocket-propelled grenades]. Every, mission we had to feel out what worked, making up doctrine as we went.

As the comments above suggest, uncertainty surrounding deployment dates and job requirements extended through all aspects of deployment and complicated the missions of military personnel in our focus groups. While some instances of uncertainty can be addressed relatively easily through an improved information-diffusion system, others are more complicated and may require revised training programs similar to those the military is currently designing and implementing to better prepare military personnel for some of the unexpected demands of nontraditional combat.

Separation from Family and Friends

For many service members with whom we spoke, separation from family and friends was cited as the most difficult and negative aspect of deployment. Many noted that being apart from their families for long periods reduced their morale and was the main reason that they did not want to deploy more often. For some focus group participants, the amount of family separation required under today's operational tempo was enough to cause them to either consider leaving or decide to leave the military. For others, although family separation was a source of considerable angst and stress, it was not yet sufficient to force the member out of the service. Personnel reported that family-separation stressors not only affected them but also their children, their spouses, and their family relationships. In some cases, military personnel also noted that their wives moved back home, to live with their parents while the member was deployed. This type of move served several purposes, including giving the wife a more stable support network and a possible child care option and reducing family expenses during the deployment. Single service members reported less stress over family separation, but still noted that it was difficult to be away from those they loved for long periods of time:

I think you will have more divorces. The deployments are killing people. You don't see your kids, and you are home just long enough to knock your wife up. It's a lot of stress on the family . . . .

When I joined the Air Force, I didn't realize that I would be deployed this often. I'm going to leave the Air Force because of deployments. Now I am married and have a kid and I want to be there for my kid.

I am married and have two boys, but I still want to deploy. Although it is hard to leave, if Iraq is the only game in town, you have to go in. . . . The choice between deployment and marriage would be hard.

Related to separation from family is the issue of communication home, which was mentioned previously in the review of military sociology. In general, personnel reported that, on deployment, they valued all forms of communication home and wished that more-frequent and more-reliable communication channels were offered. Service members noted that phones and email services are often not working, even on routine deployments. The situation was even worse in cases like Iraq, where bases first had to be built to support phone and email communications. Although service members who had been on these deployments reported that they had more access to phones as bases became more established, they commented that even when phone service was provided, long lines, frequent disconnections, and high cost continued to make communication home a challenge.

Mail service was available in most locations, but it was described as very slow. We heard that it would often take months for letters from the United States to reach them in Iraq. Lack of communication home, particularly when such communication had been expected by service members, was described as having a dampening effect on morale for most members, and, for some, it was a significant source of stress:

We started calling "the morale phones" de-morale phones, because they never worked. You could spend hours getting through, and when you finally do, the phone goes down.

First six months we had basically no communication home. Even once communications were set up, there was a 2- to 3-hour wait to use the phone.

People had to write letters, and the mail service was terrible. I couldn't get any mail for the first three months, and I was worried how things were back home with my wife. I couldn't keep my food down.

However, some focus group participants did not want more-frequent communication home. Some members with whom we spoke felt that talking to family while on deployment only increased homesickness and caused distraction from the mission at hand, especially when communication brought bad or unwanted news:

> I didn't call often. I didn't want to deal with it. I'd just end up missing my family more.

> Email and phone help a little bit. But they can be a distraction from work. You might get news at sea that you don't want to hear.

Separation from family appears to be a significant negative aspect of deployment for service members and one that causes them and their families hardship, leading to negative reenlistment for some. At the same time, however, some personnel in our focus groups still wanted to deploy, out of a sense of duty and mission, despite the difficulty of family separation. These findings are again consistent with the model in Chapter Two: Although family separation may factor in negatively to the overall utility of members, other positive aspects of deployment may act to offset the effects of separation when it comes to making the final reenlistment decision. The comments above also suggest that, although communication home is not a morale booster for all service members, more-frequent contact with family and loved ones was an important concern of many of the service members with whom we spoke. To the extent that better communication home can reduce the stress caused by family separation, communication might be a worthwhile area on which military leadership should focus its attention.

Reintegration and Readjustment

Stressors to deployed military personnel and their families exist even after the deployment has ended and the military member has returned home. Service members reported that reintegrating themselves into their families and communities and readjusting to civilian life were also challenges that they had to face. Reintegration with family was reported as a significant source of stress for married personnel. Service members across all services had to deal with changes that had occurred in the family since they left and reestablish their relationships with their children and spouses. Some noted that their very young children no longer recognized them when they returned from duty. Others reported that it was a challenge to get back into the "team mind-set" with their spouses and that they had to renegotiate the "power-sharing" relationship in the family. Most focus group members who spoke about family reintegration problems noted that, with time, things tended to improve:

> I'm trying not to just take over the house from my wife. I'm trying to gradually approach a co-level with her. I don't like it when she makes decisions without me, even though she was used to doing it while I was away.

> Deployments are hard on families because life goes on without the deployed person and, when he comes back, he is changed.

> It's slowly getting better. My kid was six months when I left and he doesn't know who I am. He doesn't want anything to do with me. When he's told to go to Daddy, he runs to the picture on the refrigerator. But things have been getting better over the past three months.

Although less of an issue for most Air Force and Navy personnel who deployed primarily on routine deployments, for those returning from hostile areas, readjustment to civilian life was often stressful. Personnel in our focus groups commented that it was difficult for them to shed some habits that they acquired while on deployment—for example, always keeping their weapons with them and scanning roads for IEDs (improvised explosive devices). Even Navy and Air Force personnel noted that it was sometimes difficult to adjust to life at home after months of being on a ship or at a forward base.

Personnel in our focus groups who had returned from hostile situations reported that it was challenging to get used to being around people again. Months after returning from Iraq, some still found it hard to be in large crowds, because, in Iraq, being in a large crowd could be very dangerous. Some of those who reported having readjustment problems noted that flashbacks and nightmares still plagued them. Others commented that they felt more short-tempered and often and easily angered. Some instances of individuals acting out, through drinking or fighting, upon return from deployment were also mentioned:

> The quiet time with my family is too quiet now. You miss life on the front when you return home.

> It's hard to adjust to not having my weapon with me. Without it I feel uncertain, unsafe. I'm not afraid to die; I've just accepted that I might. I almost did get blown up a few times.

> People were having trouble sleeping. I had a dream about being captured and tied up by Iraqis. I was going to be beheaded. I started freaking out when I woke up and looked for my pistol.

> I have more rage, more arguments with my wife over dumb things. I could imagine killing someone who cut me off on the road. I flip out for stupid reasons.

The military offers some services for personnel returning from deployment, targeted at helping them to reintegrate into their civilian lives more easily. According to focus group participants, reintegration briefings given to personnel before they are allowed to return to their families, and sometimes for extended periods of time after they return, advise service members on how to effectively immerse themselves in their families and civilian communities. Personnel are warned that their children may not recognize them and are told that they should not try to immediately take some control back from their spouses, who have become used to managing the household. They are told not to drive too fast, something they may have become accustomed to doing in Iraq. Furthermore, service members are given the opportunity to talk about their feelings, concerns, or experiences, as a type of therapeutic release.

Many of the service members who mentioned the reintegration briefings found them useful in the readjustment process. However, many also noted that they were somewhat uncomfortable discussing their feelings or fears in this type of forum. Still others were more skeptical of the value of the reintegration briefings or felt that the briefings did not go far enough in offering counseling and support to service members:

> [In the reintegration briefings] If you're married, they tell you when you come back what to expect, how long it takes, and so forth. I've been back four months and I'm still trying to catch up on what I missed. That's a year I'll never get back.

> They just give a [reintegration] briefing so that they can check the block. It's really just so that the Army can [be covered] in case something happens. It's really what you already know. It could be better, could go much more in depth.

The comments above reinforce the fact that, for our focus group participants, the stress associated with deployment did not end with the return to the United States; instead, it involved a protracted period of reintegration and reacclimatization to civilian life. Importantly, some of the challenges faced by personnel (flashbacks, nightmares, anger) could be signs of more serious mental illnesses. Military health officials are currently addressing the potential mental health consequences of long and hostile deployments. The reintegration briefings discussed above are one example of this effort. Our focus group comments suggest the importance of these types of initiatives.

Deployment Stressors for the Nondeployed

Although our conversations focused primarily on deployment-related topics, we were also interested more generally in how increased deployment frequency and tempo affect those who do not deploy and those who support missions from the home base.

Our discussions suggested that the increase in operational tempo has affected the lives of most military personnel, including those who remain behind. Personnel who have not deployed ever or at least who remained at home during Operation Iraqi Freedom reported several stressors that they faced as a result of recent deployments—increased workload and work pace being uppermost. Importantly, it is possible that the contradiction mentioned at the start of this chapter—that despite difficult deployment conditions, personnel who deploy are more likely to reenlist than those who do not—can be explained, in part, by the negative conditions experienced by nondeployed personnel at home base. Negative aspects of nondeployed life may reduce the reenlistment rates of nondeployed personnel, just as positive aspects of deployment may increase the reenlistment rates of those deployed.

Increased Workload and Work Pace

Military personnel who did not deploy still reported that increases in operational tempo have affected their workload, in the form of longer work hours and increased work pace. Some of this increased workload is associated with preparing units for deployment and supporting units that are already deployed. For example, nondeployed personnel reported carrying out medical checks, gear checks, equipment maintenance, and information processing/administration tasks for those personnel who are deployed.

Work pace and hours are also increased as a result of reduced manning caused when deployed personnel leave their positions and no one comes to take their place. We heard in focus groups across all services that, when a shop or department loses people to deployment, those remaining behind are forced to assume additional responsibilities, which often leads to longer workdays and more deadline pressure. According to focus group participants, this problem is sometimes exacerbated because the most experienced people are the ones who deploy (at least this is what some focus group members perceived), leaving less-experienced personnel, who may lack sufficient training, to pick up the slack.

Some personnel, particularly in the Air Force, complained that undermanning (i.e., when a unit has fewer personnel than it was programmed to have) throughout the service contributes to the problem. Nondeployed personnel in our focus groups reported that, when personnel from their base deployed, they frequently had to work more than 12 hours per day, sometimes on weekends, and that their schedules were often unpredictable. Non-deployed personnel were not unwilling to assume extra work, but some were resentful that they received no recognition, in the form of additional compensation or the respect given to returning deployed personnel, for their extra sacrifice, as those who deployed did.

Finally, it is worth noting that, although most personnel felt that their on-base duties contributed to the greater mission, some focus group participants, particularly junior members, complained that they did not feel that they were doing the type of work they signed up to do and that often they were forced to work for long hours on seemingly unimportant tasks:

> In my specialty, all the information from the deployed theater has to be processed, and there are fewer people on base to do the work.

> In Medical, we have to clear those who will deploy. Most of these appointments aren't planned, they will just tell you that "you need to do this now." You have more rush cases before deployments.

> Operational tempo rises a lot when people are on deployment. People deploy, but [at home] we don't get replacements. One person may end up doing the work of three people.

> Even when people deploy, you still have telephones and network accounts to handle—that doesn't go away. But there are fewer people around to take care of things. And the backlog keeps growing. You can't recover enough, given the increased rate of deployments.

> Another aspect of this problem is that when they send experienced personnel away, we are left with the same workload and lower-quality personnel. This makes it hard to complete the work.

> Marines are a CAN DO force. It is accepted that the Marines do more with less . . . Marines "don't ask for a lot of people, but ask a lot from their people."

Not only is this work pace physically exhausting, but, according to focus group participants, it takes service members away from their families for long periods of time. Although the service member is technically at home, nondeployed personnel we spoke to said that, for their families, long work hours and extended workweeks amounted to an absence akin to deploying. This family separation due to long hours also caused stress and dissatisfaction among focus group participants:

> Having to work overtime every day like I do hurts my family life because I miss out on everything at home.

> Working hours like I do, I am missing out on my kid's life. I don't have time, and my family doesn't understand.

The comments above emphasize the extent to which increased operational tempo affects the work hours, work pace, and associated work stress levels of those left behind. In general, focus group participants who had not deployed reported that deployments increased their workload, both because of the amount of work required to support deployed operations and because of personnel shortages caused when a large number of personnel deploy. Although this finding is not surprising, it does add insight to a discussion of the effects of deployment on the morale and attitudes of military personnel in general.

Reintegration with Returning Deployed

Another stressor mentioned by some nondeployed personnel in our focus groups was the challenge of reintegrating with returning deployed personnel. This theme emerged primarily among Army and Marine personnel. According to focus group participants, troops who have been deployed together, often in difficult and life-threatening situations, form strong bonds that are unlike those they share with nondeployed personnel, even if those nondeployed personnel were in their unit before the deployment. Some nondeployed personnel reported facing mild resentment from their colleagues who had deployed and felt that the nondeployed had "shirked" their duty in some way.

Several nondeployed personnel and personnel who joined a unit following the unit's return from deployment also commented that it was sometimes difficult for them to be fully accepted as a member of the unit, either because the bonds of the returning were too tight and exclusive or because returning deployed personnel all shared a similar way of thinking or set of defining experiences.

Finally, nondeploying NCOs reported that it was sometimes difficult for them to assert their authority over subordinates who had deployed or to conduct training from a manual for guys who had been using their skills in combat in Iraq for six months. Interestingly, the issue of a gap between combat soldiers and those who have not deployed is one that has emerged in the context of previous conflicts, as well (Kellet, 1982).

It is important to note, however, that while some nondeployed personnel in our focus groups did cite the gap between deployed and nondeployed as a source of stress or concern, the majority of nondeployed personnel with whom we spoke did not think that reintegration was a significant or insurmountable problem. As in the case of reintegration with family, most nondeployed personnel reported that, with time, the gap between themselves and their deploying colleagues tended to fade:

> I was in Afghanistan, but since I wasn't deployed in this rotation, they think I'm a dog even though I have more combat zone experiences. It's like being a "leg" in an airborne unit . . . .

> The new guys who've come into the platoon find it hard. They feel left out, like they're on the outside.

> People accept me, but I can't help but feel that everyone who has gone, they're all tight and how can they not resent you for not being there? . . . They've seen things that change how they think, so you have to be able to understand them.

> My troop has been pretty accepting of me. There are a few people who resent me, but most don't. I was supposed to be part of a group that is in Iraq now, but something happened.

> We can learn some little stuff from the guys who have already been deployed, like mission-specific uses of equipment and familiarity about equipment. We expected the divide between green and tan to be much worse.[2]

> It's hard to tell service members I outrank what to do in a class on things they've already done in combat and I haven't. I've been shunned in that way.

The comments presented above provide several examples of the gap that tends to emerge between deployed and nondeployed personnel. Although most nondeployed personnel felt that this challenge was relatively easy to overcome, several of the statements suggest that at least some nondeployed personnel feel that the gap between deployed and nondeployed personnel increases the stress present in their work environment and may contribute to negative reenlistment intentions for some service members.

---

[2] Green uniform = nondeployed, Tan uniform = deployed to the desert.

Benefits of Deployment

Although deployments involve significant stressors, including long work hours, high work pace, uncertainty, separation from family and friends, and exposure to danger, service members we interviewed cited many positive aspects of deployment. These aspects may play an important role in explaining the counterintuitive relationship between deployments and reenlistment rates mentioned earlier by offsetting some of the more-negative deployment experiences in the minds and attitudes of military personnel. The most frequently mentioned benefits of deployment were the opportunity to participate in challenging and fulfilling real-world missions, the development of strong friendships and interpersonal bonds, and financial gain.

Participation in Challenging, Fulfilling Work

Probably the most frequently cited positive aspect of deployment in our focus groups was the opportunity on deployments to apply training and preparation to real-world situations and to participate in challenging and satisfying missions. Focus group members reported that they derived a sense of fulfillment from their work on deployments that they did not get from conducting training exercises or daily work at home. Participants also commented that training exercises and other activities on base were often micromanaged by senior officers and focused primarily on protocol, whereas, on deployments, work was more challenging and attention was focused on accomplishing the larger mission at hand.

Many focus group participants reported returning home with a sense of accomplishment, one that increased their enjoyment of deployments, both because they had completed their jobs well and because they believed that they had contributed to a larger purpose—for example, building schools or distributing food to Iraqi or Afghani civilians. Several members who had returned from Iraq said they felt a sense of pride after returning from their deployment, because they had quickly learned and become proficient at a range of tasks for which they were not trained explicitly:

> I wanted to get deployed and get combat experience. The best part of my job is getting to work in a combat situation and knowing that I made aircraft fly. This is what I joined the Marines for and trained for.

> I kind of wanted to go because I really got to do my job. You don't want to just stay in the garrison all the time and never do the real thing. It would be like my sister going to nursing school and then not becoming a nurse.

> You get a sense of accomplishment, especially when the plane returns with the bombs you loaded gone, meaning you did your job right and protected the pilots, enabled the mission.

> I felt like I was doing something more important. I haven't been home for more than two months since 9/11, and I don't consider that a negative. You're part of something bigger than yourself.

The comments above offer insight into what service members view as some of the positive attributes of their work requirements and duties while on deployment, including the opportunity to use preparation and training, to participate in meaningful and important missions, and to accomplish something significant. These are characteristics of deployment that are likely to factor positively into the individual's overall utility. Interestingly, many service members said that work intensity and pace were both a source of stress and a source of challenge and personal accomplishment.

Camaraderie and Unit Cohesion

Another positive aspect of deployment that was discussed by many focus group participants in all services was the chance to form strong bonds with colleagues and coworkers. Cohesion was discussed extensively in Chapter Two in the context of both sociology literature and psychology literature. Personnel with whom we spoke noted that shared experiences and trials on deployment contributed to increased unit cohesion and camaraderie that lasted beyond the end of the deployment and was highly valued by service members. Focus group participants commented that, while on a long deployment, a member's unit becomes like his family. As a result, members come to rely on each other for support, comfort, and survival. Although this is particularly true on deployments involving exposure to danger, increased cohesion was cited as a positive aspect of nonhostile deployments, as well:

> We really had to draw on each other for strength—the people you were with all the time, the people you bonded to.

> You become like a family.

> You see people from all walks of life pull together. It's unbelievable to see it happen. All those personalities put aside for a task and you see them succeed at it.

> I feel like I have 135 close friends that I didn't have before I went to Iraq.

The statements above emphasize the positive effect that deployment has on unit cohesion and highlight long-term friendships and camaraderie as a positive aspect of deployment, one that improves the deployment experience. Unit cohesion serves a significant purpose for personnel on deployment, forming a network that provides deployed personnel with physical, mental, and emotional support systems.

Financial Gain

Financial gain was a final significant positive aspect of deployment mentioned by focus group members. Military personnel receive additional compensation for serving overseas, including Family Separation Pay, Hostile Fire Pay, and some tax exemptions, all of which increase the total income of service members sent on deployments.[3] Deployed troops save money further simply because there is usually little to buy during military operations and basic needs are provided by the service. Service members with whom we spoke reported that special and incentive pays constitute a significant addition to their incomes, especially for Army and Marine personnel who were deployed to combat zones and could take full advantage of the special pays offered.

For some, the financial incentive was so significant that members commented that they preferred to deploy, considering family separation a manageable price to pay for the additional money. However, some service members were less enthusiastic about the monetary benefit, noting that it was nice to get extra money, but that the money was not enough to make them want to go on deployment.

Members in our focus groups reported using the extra money for a range of purposes, including buying big-ticket items such as cars or TVs, paying off credit-card debt or other loans, or saving the money for future investment. Importantly, focus group participants felt that additional pay and the purchases made with this extra pay are also benefits of deployment that can be shared by the service member's family and help offset some of their hardships:

> The pay was good. It was tax-free, and I got Family Separation Pay. My pay was twice as much as when I'm here.

> Besides the negative of being away from family, we want to deploy. We can save money and get separation pay of $250 per month and danger pay. Single Marines definitely would rather deploy. They can save even more money because they have fewer expenses. . . . The added money is [a] factor.

> I liked the money. I paid off all my bills and saved money, too. But I'd rather not go to Iraq to make money—it's not a reason to go.

> The money was good, and when I got back my husband had paid off all our credit cards. This type of thing helps family members understand the deployment.

The comments above suggest the effectiveness of financial incentives in offsetting some of the negative aspects of long military deployments, particularly when the financial incentives are large compared with the member's base pay. These findings correspond to the implications from the utility model—specifically, that monetary incentives are likely to increase member utility and contribute to an upward revision of expected utility from deployment.

---

[3] Members with dependents receive a family separation allowance for absences over 30 consecutive days (there is no equivalent for single members without children). Additional pay is provided for serving in designated "hostile areas," and income earned in a "combat zone," including reenlistment bonuses, is tax-free. The tax exemption is unlimited for enlisted personnel and warrant officers, and it is limited to $78,350.40 for officers. This limit usually affects only senior officers.

However, for many members in our focus groups, although financial benefits of deployments may reduce the pain of such stressors as family separation and long work hours, they are unlikely to completely eliminate the negative effects of deployment on personnel morale and attitudes.

Moderators: Dealing with Stress on Deployments

Our focus group discussions also covered the types of resources that military personnel found useful in dealing with stressors encountered on deployments, both hostile and nonhostile. As was discussed in Chapter Two, factors or programs that reduce the effect of stressors on individuals are known as *moderators*. Focus group participants identified several key moderators that they felt helped them to perform effectively on deployment, despite physical challenges, uncertainty, and long work hours.

The most commonly discussed stress moderators included training (which was discussed as an important moderator according to relevant literature, in Chapter Two) and talking with colleagues and commanders.

Training

Throughout our focus groups, training emerged as a factor that helped military personnel deal with and respond to the challenges of their deployments. Furthermore, because of their effectiveness when they were appropriately designed to include relevant skills and challenges, existing training programs were perceived by many focus group members to need revising and expanding to more accurately reflect the demands of nontraditional and other deployments.

In general, despite the existence of some job-related uncertainty discussed in a previous section of this chapter, military personnel felt that their training was effective in preparing them for most of the requirements and duties of deployment. Focus group participants, especially those in the Navy and Air Force whose deployments tended to conform more closely to traditional and predicted patterns, noted that field exercises and other drills provided members with many of the skills needed to successfully perform on deployments.

Feeling prepared to do their jobs and handle challenging situations helped the service members with whom we spoke to maintain high levels of performance, even under stressful circumstances:

> A lot of my training was useful—going out to gather intel, tactical checkpoints, minefields.

> We get drilled on certain situations. The more you drill, the better you can handle things.

> What you're doing is dangerous . . . . It's a reason that training is important. It helps you control the danger.

It's hard to prepare you for all the types of deployments. You do get cultural briefings, and those are good. It has taken me several TDYs [temporary duties] and deployments to really adapt to deployments. For people on their first and second deployments, they may need more training and practice; but even that won't be a
cure-all. You have to know your job; that helps a lot.

However, focus group members, particularly in the Army and Marines, also noted
that existing training did not address all of the demands and requirements of nontraditional
warfare. For example, Army and Marine personnel felt that they lacked training relevant to
dealing with an insurgency-type attack or conducting urban combat operations (carrying out
house-to-house raids, operating border checkpoints, etc.), as well as peacekeeping operations.
They noted that the development and application of training based on lessons learned in Iraq
and Afghanistan would be helpful in eliminating some of the stressors associated with Iraq
operations and deployments for future deployed personnel.

Focus group participants mentioned cultural and language training as one area in
which further preparation would increase the beneficial effect of training on stress reduction.
Other areas for which additional training is needed, according to focus group participants,
include peacekeeping skills, conducting searches and raids, and taking hostages:

We're trained to fight an enemy that shows itself, but in Iraq it was unconventional
warfare.

We were basically doing guerrilla warfare. Everyone had some training on how to
clear a building, maybe a day's worth, but not on patrolling and fighting in city
streets. We needed more of this type of training.

Language classes and basic Arabic skills [customs and culture] are needed. You pick
up some Arabic while you're there.

I don't feel I had peacekeeping skills or the police skills needed to do security duty.

Importantly, since the time of our focus groups, the military services have taken significant steps toward updating and revising their training programs to better prepare individuals for the demands of nontraditional deployments.

The comments above underscore the importance that focus group participants placed
on training as a tool that military planners can use to prepare service members for the stressors and challenges of deployment. Not only did service members with whom we spoke believe that training had contributed to the successful completion of their missions, but they
expressed a desire for new types of training based on the realities of current and future deployments. Importantly, as mentioned previously, despite some job uncertainty and training
gaps, military personnel felt able to adapt to the demands of deployment and become proficient at new tasks, sometimes as a direct result of their military training and predeployment

preparation. This gaining of proficiency represents another way in which training served as a moderator for deployed personnel and helped them deal with the work stress on deployment.

It is worth noting that several focus group participants mentioned that, because of long deployments, training cycles were often disrupted and personnel were unable to get the training and preparation that they needed to be promoted or simply to be prepared for future operations. Finally, some focus group discussants noted that their preparation was negatively affected by lack of proper equipment and protective gear. This is an issue that the military is aware of and is addressing.

Talking to Friends, Chaplains, and Mental Health Teams

According to our focus group participants, the most helpful mechanism for coping with stress on deployment was talking with other unit members and commanders. Personnel with whom we spoke noted that they derived the most benefit from expressing their feelings and describing their experiences to other service members who had been through the same experiences, rather than talking to an "outsider" who might not be able to relate directly. Furthermore, as mentioned above, unit cohesion and connection between members on deployment was extremely strong. Many members shared everything within their units, including fears and emotional reactions to specific events.

In our groups, most members preferred talking with colleagues to seeking help from a chaplain or a mental health professional, for several reasons. First, as mentioned above, members found it more helpful to talk to friends who had common experiences than to talk to a removed third party. Second, although chaplains and mental health professionals were generally available to personnel who needed or wanted to utilize them as formal helping resources (this was less true for those deployed in remote areas, particularly early during Operation Iraqi Freedom), focus group members reported that there is a certain stigma attached to those who sought out emotional or psychological counseling. Personnel with whom we spoke noted that sometimes, asking for help is associated with weakness. Service members in our groups perceived that this "weakness" can affect an individual's reputation and promotion potential, despite service statements to the contrary and promises of confidentiality. As a result, personnel reported being hesitant to actively seek out more-formal types of counseling.

Some service members reported participating in postdeployment counseling sessions with their units soon after their return to the United States. Although several of the focus group participants who mentioned this type of counseling found it useful, others were more skeptical and noted that the military could do a better job of offering counseling to returning soldiers:

> If I needed help, I would be more likely to turn to other unit members. We can talk it out amongst ourselves.

> Counseling could be much better. Instead, it is just a short briefing so the Army can check a block.

> Asking for help is seen as cowardice, so you don't like to bring up the fact that you might need help.

> The combat stress team is not helpful at all. They weren't there in the situation with you. Your buddy is more helpful.

> They publicize mental health services . . . but people are better off not going unless you are told to because it will hurt your career . . . .

As indicated by the comments above, service members tended to rely on each other for support when dealing with difficult or stressful situations, because such support was the most helpful, direct, and appealing counseling option open to them. Although more-formal briefings and stress-management programs do exist, most focus group members did not use these services either, because they felt that they had no need, because they did not expect these programs to be helpful, or because they were concerned about the stigma associated with seeking mental health counseling.

Other Moderators

In the course of our discussions, service members reported using several other types of stress moderators to deal with the stressors faced on deployment, including exercise/PT (physical training), entertainment (video games and movies), and communication with family members at home. Other members noted that rest and relaxation (R&R) mid-deployment breaks were helpful in relieving stress, but made it much more difficult to return to the theater. Finally, many personnel with whom we spoke took 30-day block leave, which was offered to many units when they returned from long deployments to Iraq, a break that helped relieve their fatigue and reduce their stress.

Summary

Our focus groups highlighted several key themes concerning the positive and negative aspects of deployment, for personnel across all services. According to focus group members, stress related to deployment exists both for those who deploy and for those who do not deploy. Among those participants who had deployed, preparation stress, operational tempo, work pace and hours on deployment, exposure to physical challenges and danger, uncertainty, and family separation and later reintegration were some of the most significant stressors. For nondeployed personnel, increased workload from having to provide necessary deployment support and from making up for personnel shortages, the resulting time away from family, and the challenges of reintegrating with returning deployed personnel were cited as factors that caused stress and made working conditions at home base more difficult. Importantly, as we discuss in the next chapter, our analysis of data from Status of Forces surveys of service members from all services confirms a link between extended work hours and increased levels of reported work and personal stress. For some personnel in our focus groups, increases in deployments, long work hours, and long periods of time away from family were contributing to their decision to leave the military.

Our focus group discussions suggest that, in order to reduce the negative effects of deployments on personnel and morale, two areas that policymakers might concentrate on are improving communication home and revising training programs to better prepare personnel for nontraditional warfare and other activities in the theater of operations. Improved communication home could help alleviate some of the stress caused by family separation; improved training could reduce uncertainty and increase a member's ability to deal with challenging situations. Importantly, military planners are already taking steps in these directions, by updating training with lessons learned in Iraq and making efforts to improve communication access for deployed personnel.

However, although focus group members reported several negative aspects of deployment and military work life, in many cases, these negatives did not translate into negative reenlistment intentions. Many focus group participants expressed a desire to stay in the service, despite the strain that increased operational tempo, long work hours, and time away from home caused. Some service members with whom we spoke who were planning to stay noted that, although deployments are difficult, they have positive aspects that offset some of these challenges—for example, financial gain, the opportunity to use skills in a real-world mission and participate in fulfilling work, and the ability to form strong interpersonal bonds with other unit members. They also noted that receiving good training and being able to rely on their colleagues for support helped them through difficult situations and challenges. These positive aspects improved their deployment experiences and their attitudes toward deployment. On the other hand, some nondeployed personnel in our focus groups reported that negative experiences associated with not deploying contributed to their negative reenlistment intentions.

It is likely that both these effects—of positive aspects of deployment on the retention intentions of deployed personnel and of negative aspects of nondeployment life on the reenlistment attitudes of nondeployed personnel—help to explain the finding that personnel who deploy tend to have higher retention rates than personnel who do not. Given this possible relationship, military planners should seek to exploit positive aspects of deployment for deployed personnel and try to extend some of these benefits to nondeployed personnel, because such actions might improve morale both on deployments and at home base.

Our focus group data are useful in offering a direct view into the deployment experiences and perceptions of the military personnel in our focus groups and help to elaborate on the utility model discussed in Chapter Two. In general, the effect of deployment on the reenlistment intentions of focus group members seemed to be mixed, and it would be difficult to draw any firm conclusions about the effect of deployments and operational tempo on future reenlistment rates. The next chapter looks at data from surveys conducted among military personnel and will offer a complementary perspective to some of the same issues discussed here.

CHAPTER FOUR

Analysis of Survey Data: Higher-Than-Usual Stress, Reenlistment Intention, and Deployments

To examine the extent to which we can generalize our qualitative findings from focus groups to the military population as a whole, we sought a large-scale survey of a randomly selected service population with questions related to our topic. The Defense Manpower Data Center (DMDC) Status of Forces Surveys of Active Duty Personnel for March 2003 and July 2003 contain the best survey data available. These periodic surveys are given to random samples of the active-duty population and aim to provide timely data on a range of personnel issues.

DMDC weighted the respondents to be representative of the active-duty population. Response rates were 35 percent for both the March 2003 survey (10,828 respondents) and the July 2003 survey (10,284 respondents). Many of the survey items we selected correspond closely with the issues explored in the focus group sessions, enabling us to draw connections between our qualitative and quantitative analyses and provide additional support for our focus group observations.[1]

The chapter is organized into three parts. We first discuss the variables we analyzed and the empirical methods we used. This discussion is followed by discussions of the empirical findings for high-than-usual work stress and for intention to stay on active duty. We then offer conclusions.

Tabulations and Predictions from the Regressions

The tabulations in this monograph are based on weighted data, and the regressions are based on unweighted data, but with weighting-related variables included in the regression specification and the data grouping used for the regressions (branch of service, enlisted/officer).[2] Separate regressions were run for each group, and the regressions included indicators for senior/junior rank, marital status, gender, and white only/minority or mixed.[3]

---

[1] It is possible that the surveys have a response bias, but we do not know; this type of bias is discussed somewhat further in Appendix B. One might conjecture that the response rate is higher among service members with a strong viewpoint on some aspect of service life that they want to communicate to military leaders. Because members could hold strong opinions on any number of aspects of service life, differing from member to member, there may be little response bias under this conjecture. Responses would not necessarily be higher among members with a positive intention to stay in the military, or among members with a negative intention to stay, or related in a systematic way to the variables included in our analysis.

[2] We also estimated regressions for data further subdivided by junior/senior. These results showed little difference between junior and senior personnel and are not reported.

[3] Respondents could indicate their race/ethnicity by marking one *or more* of the following: white, black or African American, American Indian or Alaska native, Asian, and native Hawaiian or other Pacific Islander.

Overall, we estimated regressions for six dependent variables: higher-than-usual personal stress; higher-than-usual work stress; likely to stay on active duty; likely to stay on active duty for 20 or more years; being away from permanent duty station in the past 12 months, or lack thereof,[4] increased your desire to stay; and (in your opinion) your spouse thinks you should stay on active duty. The personal-stress and work-stress regressions were similar, and the work-stress regression fit the data better.[5] Also, the regression for intention to stay on active duty fit the data better than did the other intention regressions. Because on net we think the most informative regressions are those on work stress and intention to stay, we present these regression results in Appendix B and use them to predict probabilities in the tables below. However, Table 4.6 provides some comparison of the statistical significance of regression results for the different measures of intention.

We coded higher-than-usual work stress if the respondent reported that work stress was "higher" or "much higher" than usual. Because this is a self-referenced measure of stress, we have been careful not to interpret it as an absolute measure of stress based on an external scale. A person can have higher-than-usual stress and yet have a low, or high, absolute level of stress. That is, higher-than-usual stress should not be interpreted as meaning "high stress."

Our explanatory variables were related to factors discussed in the model and literature review in Chapter Two and in the focus groups:

- Number of times worked longer-than-usual duty-day in past 12 months (0, 1–10, 11–20, 21–60, 61–120, >120)
- Away from permanent duty station in past 12 months (yes/no)
- Interaction of "away" with indicators for number of times worked longer than usual duty-day
- Involved in combat operations in Afghanistan (OEF) or Iraq (OIF) in the 12 months prior to July–August 2003
- Away more or less time than expected (much less, less, neither more nor less, more, much more)
- Individual prepared for wartime job (very well, well, neither well nor poorly, poorly, very poorly)
- Unit prepared for its wartime mission (very well, well, neither well nor poorly, poorly, very poorly).

We also included the following demographic variables:

- Service (Army, Navy, Marines, Air Force)
- Seniority (E-5 through E-9 if enlisted, O-4 to O-6 if officer)
- Marital status

---

[4] The wording "time away (or lack thereof)" may seem puzzling, but because the question was asked of everyone, the wording was chosen, we think, to accommodate the possibility that either being away or not being away could affect career intention.

[5] We base this statement on the higher R-squared and higher F-tests for sets of explanatory variables included in the work-stress regression compared with the personal-stress regression.

- Gender
- Majority/minority race.

The omitted group categories in the regressions are as follows: worked longer than the usual duty-day zero to 20 times; not away; not in OEF/OIF combat operations; time away was neither more nor less than expected; you feel neither well nor poorly prepared; your unit is neither well nor poorly prepared; junior rank (E-1–E-4; O-1–O-3); not married; male; and self-reported race/ethnicity is white only.

We tabulated means for the various regressions and groups (Appendix B).[6] The means differed across the regressions, but the differences were slight.[7] We therefore present means only from the stress regressions sample, and we also include means of the dependent variables from the other regressions. The means are based on weighted data. There is virtually no difference between the weighted and unweighted means for the explanatory variables, except for the variables indicating senior rank, married, female, and nonwhite. Even though the regressions were estimated on unweighted data, we thought it would be most helpful to the reader to have the weighted means, because they are representative of the population and more useful for prediction.

We estimated linear probability models.[8] It was clear from cross-tabulations that the probability of the event lay in the linear part of the cumulative distribution function[9] in most cases. Thus, the results of the linear probability model are close to those of a bell-curve model, such as the logistic or probit, and the linear coefficients are easy for computing probabilities should the reader want to do additional computations and/or predictions. The predicted probabilities in the tables below use the omitted group as the base.

The explanatory variables are intended to represent circumstances that are largely outside the service member's control, or exogenous. This distinction is important in the empirical analysis; if the individual had control over the explanatory variables, they would be endogenous. For instance, if service members have no choice over whether they work longer than the usual duty-day, then our analysis allows us to infer how changes in the number of times a member works longer than the usual duty-day affect his intention to stay. But, if the member can choose duty-day length, then a negative "effect" of working longer on intention to stay could instead represent a preference among members with low intention to choose long duty-days.

---

[6] The table of means in Appendix B does not include standard deviations. Because all the variables take the value of "0" or "1," the standard deviation of a variable equals the square root of the mean times one minus the mean. That is, if m is the mean, the standard deviation is the square root of $m (1 - m)$.

[7] Differences occurred because of slight differences in sample size arising from missing data.

[8] A *linear probability model* applies ordinary least squares to a dependent variable defined to take the value of "1" to indicate that an event has occurred (e.g., the individual reports being "likely" or "very likely" to stay in the military) and a value of "0" otherwise. The linear probability model has a linear structure; it can be written as a linear equation with an intercept and terms consisting of an explanatory variable multiplied by its coefficient. In contrast, logistic and probit probability models are nonlinear. Such models are generally preferable to the linear probability model. However, as in our case, when the response range is on a linear part of the nonlinear model, the linear probability model performs similarly to the nonlinear models. The results of the linear probability model are easy to interpret, making it appealing in our circumstances.

[9] The *cumulative distribution function* maps the probability that a random outcome x is less than or equal to a stated value X. The cumulative distribution function is s-shaped when the random variable is distributed by a bell-shaped curve—for example, normal, logistic, or binomial.

Our maintained assumption is that members had little control over the number of times they worked longer-than-usual duty-day, whether they were away from their permanent duty station in the past 12 months, and whether they served in combat operations in OEF/OIF. We recognize that, to some extent, members can exert control over their circumstances. A senior officer might set his own pace of work, for instance, with some officers working long days more often than others, even though they face the same tasking. But, in general, a member's hours of work depend on the requirements for whatever military mission is to be undertaken. As we found in the focus group discussions, aircraft maintenance personnel worked late, long hours to ready aircraft for the next day; seamen put in long days and weeks to prepare ships for deployment and meet training qualifications; and soldiers and Marines had dawn-to-dusk days of training and field exercises. Long days were common on deployment, too.

The combat indicator is based on the July 2003 survey. The survey was conducted between July 21 and August 28, 2003, and asked about the 12-month period prior to the survey. The combat question is worded as follows: "Were you involved in combat operations?" No additional information is given to the respondent about how to define "combat" or "involvement." The period covered by the survey is after the main military action in Afghanistan, but it includes smaller-scale military activities in Afghanistan, including actions against Taliban refugees in the mountains adjoining Pakistan.[10] This period also covers preparations for the war in Iraq, including predeployment training and exercises in the United States and the buildup of military resources in staging areas, such as Kuwait and offshore, as well as the major initial combat activities in Iraq. Operation Iraqi Freedom began on March 19, 2003, with air strikes followed by ground assault. Much of the fighting against Saddam Hussein's forces took place between then and April 9, followed by operations to gain stability beginning around May 1, 2003. During the 12 months the survey used as a frame of reference, relatively few personnel were killed or injured in action.[11]

The variables indicating time away relative to expectations depend on both the length of time away and on the individual's expectation of time away. The length of time away often depends on factors outside the individual's control. For instance, the service may send members away to obtain training or to participate in exercises, and the service determines the requirements for deployment to military operations. However, in some cases being sent away depends on the member. A member who wants to redeploy might need to reenlist if the date of deployment is close to the end of the member's term of service. Also, whether a

---

[10] According to Global Security, an organization that provides links to national-security articles appearing in the press and that also offers information about military operations,

> By mid-March 2002, the Taliban had been removed from power and the Al Qaida network in Afghanistan had been destroyed. The US continued to exploit detainees and sensitive sites for their intelligence value in order to prevent future terrorist attacks and to further US understanding of Al Qaida—their plans, membership, structure, and intentions. The US was investigating each site to confirm or deny the existence of research into, or production of, chemical, biological, or radiological weapons. Coalition forces continued to locate and destroy remaining pockets of Taliban and Al Qaida fighters and to search for surviving leadership.

Available online at http://www.globalsecurity.org/military/ops/enduring-freedom.htm; accessed November 29, 2004.

[11] As of November 29, 2004, there had been 148 total deaths in OEF, of which 109 were in and around Afghanistan and 39 were in other locations (e.g., Kuwait, Pakistan, Persian Gulf). There were 1,251 total deaths in OIF, of which 139 occurred in combat operations during March 19 through April 30, 2003, and 1,109 died in post–combat operations from May 1 onward. Another three deaths were U.S. Department of Defense civilian employees. See http://www.defenselink.mil/news/casualty.pdf.

member is sent to attend a course for new NCOs may depend on the member's effort to obtain promotion to sergeant.

The variables for individual and unit preparedness rely on the individual's perception of what "preparedness" means and requires. In other words, because the preparedness variables are based on self-assessments, they are not purely objective and standardized measures of preparedness, and might to some degree be co-determined with stress and intentions. *Preparedness* depends on training, experience, leadership, unit cohesion, equipment availability, and so forth, and these factors are typically beyond the individual's control. However, the perception of being well or poorly prepared might also be related to unobserved individual characteristics—for example, self-efficacy. Literature on the effects of stress on performance would lead us to believe that members with high self-efficacy might have lower stress and a higher intention to continue. As we note below, most members perceived that they and their unit are well prepared or very well prepared, and only 1 or 2 percent of members said that they or their unit are very poorly prepared.

We excluded stress from the intention regressions and intention variables from the stress regressions because stress and intention are likely to be simultaneously determined by the same variables. We had no way of identifying their separate effects on each other, and including them as explanatory variables could have biased the regression coefficient estimates.[12]

Findings on Higher-Than-Usual Work Stress

Frequent Long Duty-Days Led to Higher-Than-Usual Work Stress

Nearly all service members reported instances of working longer than their usual duty-day in the past 12 months. In fact, more than one-fourth of personnel worked longer than their usual duty-day more than 120 times in the past 12 months. This result underscores what service members told us in focus groups: that they frequently work very long and unpredictable hours. Military personnel are technically on call every day, and longer-than-usual duty-days are clearly not uncommon.[13]

We found that members who were away from their home station in the past 12 months worked longer than their usual duty-day far more frequently than did members who were not away (Figure 4.1). Forty-four percent of service members were away at some time in the past 12 months prior to the survey dates of March 2003 and July 2003, and 56 percent worked entirely at their permanent duty station. Of those with time away, 39 percent worked longer than their usual duty-day more than 120 times, compared with 19 percent of

---

[12] If one believes that the equations in the underlying model should include higher-than-usual work stress in the intention equation, and intention to stay in the higher-than-usual work-stress equation, then by excluding these variables we are, in effect, estimating a reduced form.

[13] However, because these are self-reports, we cannot be certain of how a member counted hours of work and defined a usual duty-day. A usual duty-day could be much different on deployment than at home station. When ships are under way, sailors are at their stations more than 8 hours per day, and when Marines and soldiers are in the field, their usual duty-day might be an irregular 16 hours. On deployments, where family and many other diversions do not tug at service members' time, work may be the default activity and primary setting for social interaction or email communication with friends and family, so work demand may not be the only factor influencing time spent "at work" on deployments. The survey instrument did not define "usual duty-day" but, as with involvement in combat operations, left its interpretation to the respondent.

those not away. Again, most focus group participants also reported working longer hours when deployed than when at home.

As Figure 4.1 shows, the percentage of service members who worked longer than the usual duty-day more than 120 times in the past 12 months is much higher for personnel who were away some time during the past 12 months than for those not away,[14] for both enlisted personnel and officers. However, in general, officers (44 to 55 percent) were more likely to report having worked longer than the usual duty-day more than 120 times than were enlisted personnel (30 to 40 percent). Also, it is perhaps surprising to find such a high incidence of this outcome, even for service members who were not away from their permanent duty station: 15 to 20 percent for enlisted, 25 to 35 percent for officers. Recent military operations evidently involved long duty-days for many nondeployed personnel.

In the next subsection, we test whether long duty-days have a different effect on higher-than-usual work stress and intention to stay according to whether the member was away in the past 12 months or not. Some examples of off-duty activities on deployment mentioned in the focus groups were playing video games, listening to compact discs, reading, and writing letters or making telephone calls home. That off-duty activities on deployment are much more limited than when at home is potentially a factor that would make long duty-days on deployment more stressful and less satisfying than a comparable number of long duty-days at home station. Furthermore, the deployed member is removed from family contact and can be stressed by being out of touch with daily events at home and unavailable

Figure 4.1
Percentage of Service Members Who Worked Longer Than the Usual Duty-Day More Than 120 Times in the Past 12 Months

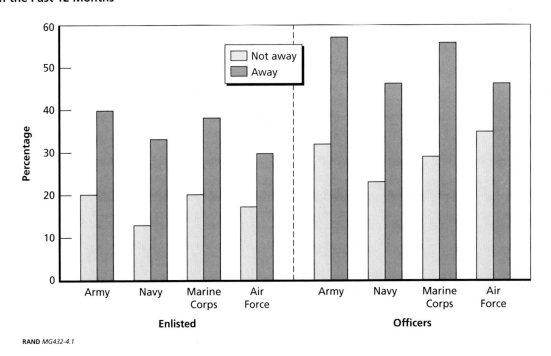

RAND *MG432-4.1*

---

[14] Appendix C presents a table of the complete distribution of the number of times service members worked longer than the usual duty-day.

to help. Still, as some focus group members mentioned, being away from home can bring relief from the stress of family problems and responsibilities.

Members Who Frequently Worked Longer Than the Usual Duty-Day Were More Likely to Have Higher-Than-Usual Work Stress

That service members who frequently worked longer than the usual duty-day were more likely to have higher-than-usual work stress is clearly seen in Figure 4.2, a survey finding that corresponds to what we heard in our focus groups. Service members with whom we spoke reported that long work hours, extended work weeks, and being forced to work overtime contributed significantly to their work stress and sometimes led to burnout. Also, although there were some differences in the stress levels for members who were away versus not away, they were minor.

The stress regression results were entirely consistent with Figure 4.2. We found that the probability of higher-than-usual work stress increased with the number of times the member worked longer than the usual duty-day. The coefficients on these indicators were highly statistically significant as a set, and the finding that stress increases with workload is consistent with the literature (Caplan and Jones, 1975; Campbell et al., 1998; Halverson, et al., 1995). When the indicator for "away" was interacted with the indicators for "worked longer," the interaction coefficients were small, indicating little difference from the coefficients for members who were not away, and the interactions were not statistically significant as a set. This result means that people not deployed are as likely to report higher-than-usual work stress as those deployed, given the same number of long duty-days.

Figure 4.2
Work Stress, by Number of Times Worked Longer Than the Usual Duty-Day

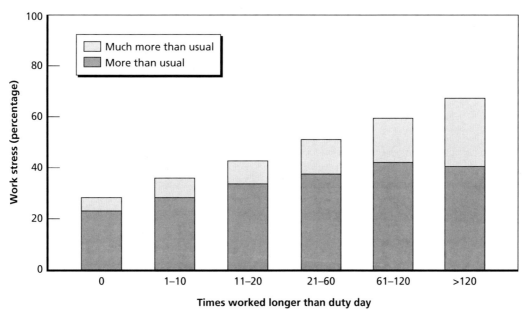

Table 4.1 shows the predicted probability of higher-than-usual work stress with respect to the number of times the member worked longer than the usual duty-day and whether or not he or she was away from his/her permanent duty station in the past year. The probability is usually higher when the number of times worked longer than the usual duty-day is 61–120 times or more than 120 times, compared with the lowest category, 0–20 times. These categories roughly correspond to long days one to two times a week and more than two times a week versus once every two weeks or less.

The relationship between longer duty-days and higher-than-usual stress was more prominent for work stress than for personal stress. The work-stress regressions fit the data better, and the worked-longer indicators were more often significant and tended to have larger coefficients. We suggest two explanations for this difference. Working longer might cause the same amount of either type of stress, but the individual considers work-related personal stress to be only one part of personal stress, the other being non-work-related stress. This consideration would dilute the perceived effect of working longer on personal stress relative to its effect on work stress. Also, work activities might create more work stress relative to personal stress. The pressure to complete a job, master a skill, or deal with a challenging situation might create work stress without creating much personal stress.

The regressions showed that the relationship between stress and the number of times the member worked longer than the usual duty-day is nearly the same for members who were away from their permanent duty station at some time during the 12 months prior to the survey as for members who were not away. This result was somewhat surprising, because being away on deployment can involve unfamiliar and harsh living conditions, a change of routine and diet, and exposure to danger. Further, Walter Reed studies list multiple sources of stress reported by deployed personnel and find that stress levels appeared to increase both with time in-theater and workload (Campbell et al., 1998; Halverson et al., 1995). Our test, however, was only a weak test of the hypothesis that stress increases more rapidly with workload on deployment than at home, because the "away" indicator in the survey tells only that the member was away at some point during the past 12 months, not for how long and where.

Table 4.1
Predicted Probability of Higher-Than-Usual Work Stress, by Worked Longer and Whether Away from Permanent Duty Station

Times worked longer than usual duty-day	Army		Navy		Marine Corps		Air Force	
	Not away	Away	Not away	Away	Not away	Away	Not away	Away
Enlisted								
0–20	.44	.42	.49	.57	.43	.37	.41	.36
21–60	.63	.62	.69	.52	.54	.65	.55	.56
61–120	.73	.66	.76	.71	.64	.57	.67	.55
>120	.75	.76	.80	.80	.71	.62	.71	.64
Officer								
0–20	.27	.23	.39	.40	.25	.28	.31	.19
21–60	.39	.28	.61	.43	.28	.34	.46	.58
61–120	.54	.42	.70	.63	.43	.37	.57	.50
>120	.64	.53	.72	.71	.59	.52	.68	.62

SOURCE: Predicted from the regressions in Appendix B.

Some members who were away might have been away for only a few days or weeks for training or an exercise, and most of their year was spent at home station. Such members would be very similar to members who were not away. By comparison, members who were actually deployed were probably away for six months or more and were likely to fall into the categories of working longer than the usual duty-day more than 120 times or, at least, more than 60 times. Therefore, we also wanted to pay close attention to the statistical significance of the away*61–120 and away*>120 interactions.

But, in almost all cases in the work-stress regressions, such interactions were not significant. The only exception was for Navy enlisted members, for whom the away*61–120 interaction indicated lower, not higher, work stress (see Appendix B). Further, with respect to the regressions for intention to stay, discussed below, the interactions were, again, not significant on the whole. The overall sense remained that being away per se was a minor factor relative to the influence of a heavy workload.

In addition, as noted in Chapter Three, we learned from focus group discussions that, for some individuals, deployments were considered less stressful than being at home, in a number of ways. The pressure of meeting training and readiness deadlines before a deployment had come to an end and personnel could simply focus on doing their jobs. Also, personnel were physically removed from their family responsibilities and the stress of day-to-day family life, although many found it difficult and stressful to stay in touch with their families because communication options were somewhat limited, costly, and unreliable.

It is worth noting, once again, that different individuals described family separation differently. While some service members reported that being away from family helped them concentrate on their jobs, others found the separation unpleasant and dissatisfying. Despite these differences at the individual level, the survey evidence indicates that a given work pace was usually no more stressful for members who were away than for those who were not away.

As discussed earlier in this monograph, focus group members reported that training and support activities related to OEF/OIF increased the frequency of working longer days for nondeployed members and increased their stress, too. Although we do not have earlier survey data to compare the number of times worked longer than usual duty-days between members who were and were not away, long duty-days have probably increased over the past five years as operating tempo has increased.

Combat Duty Had Little Effect on Higher-Than-Usual Work Stress

Involvement in combat operations in OEF/OIF in the period covered by the survey had a small effect, sometimes positive and sometimes negative, on higher-than-usual work stress and was usually not statistically significant. The results for enlisted personnel were statistically insignificant, except for the Air Force, for which the probability of higher-than-usual work stress was lower for those in combat operations than those not in combat operations. For officers, the combat indicator was significant and positive for Army officers (meaning a higher probability of higher-than-usual work stress), significant and negative for Marine officers, and insignificant in the Air Force and Navy.

Being Away Much More Time Than Expected Increased the Probability of Higher-Than-Usual Work Stress

Table 4.2 displays the predicted probability of higher-than-usual stress with respect to whether time away was much less, less, neither more nor less, more, or much more than expected. The coefficient on "much more than expected" was often statistically significant, which contributed to making the entire set of indicators significant. As can be seen, the relationship between higher than usual work stress and time away varied by group. For instance, the probability for soldiers and sailors was not lower if they were away less time than expected, relative to neither more nor less than expected, but was higher if they were away more or much more time than expected, whereas the probability was lower for Army and Marine Corps officers who were away less time than expected and higher for those who were away more time than expected.

This finding is closely related to the discussion in Chapter Three of the effects of uncertainty on personnel. As mentioned previously, personnel with whom we spoke highlighted uncertainty about deployments as an aspect of military life that leads to increased work stress. The literature on individual response to stress offers insight into these findings: Individuals appear to experience lower levels of stress and less-severe reductions in performance quality when their expectations are accurate—matching the reality. Studies suggest that additional information and training that contribute to the formation of accurate expectations[15] can help moderate the effects of stress (Johnston and Cannon-Bowers, 1996).

Table 4.2
Predicted Probability of Higher-Than-Usual Work Stress, by Whether Time Away Was Less or More Than Expected, Among Those Who Were Away

Time away relative to expected time away	Army	Navy	Marine Corps	Air Force
Enlisted				
Much less	.43	.53	.38	.40
Less	.43	.49	.45	.38
Neither	.44	.49	.43	.41
More	.52	.60	.47	.54
Much more	.55	.66	.48	.51
Officer				
Much less	.17	.37	.15	.25
Less	.23	.32	.16	.25
Neither	.27	.39	.25	.31
More	.34	.39	.33	.42
Much more	.41	.53	.35	.52

SOURCE: Predicted from regressions in Appendix B.

---

[15] An *accurate expectation* is the mean, or stable expected value, of a stable distribution describing the probability of given random events occurring in an underlying process. Individuals subject to the same random process might have their own expectations that are far different from the mean of the distribution, which are, hence, inaccurate expectations—even though they might seem accurate to the individual.

Higher-Than-Usual Work Stress Was Less Likely If the Member Felt Personally Prepared and Felt His or Her Unit Was Prepared

The probability of higher-than-usual work stress was lower for those who felt very well prepared or well prepared, and higher for those who felt very poorly prepared, as Table 4.3 shows. Additionally, the sets of individual- and unit-preparedness indicators were usually statistically significant.

The finding that the probability was lower for individuals who felt that they and their units were prepared is supported by the literature on the role that effective training can play in reducing individual responses to stress and improving performance under stress (Deikis, 1982; Saunders et al., 1996; Sheehy and Horan, 2004). It is also consistent with focus group data. As discussed in Chapter Three, personnel with whom we spoke felt that effective training helped them to perform successfully in a range of tasks and operations and allowed them to respond to challenges. They also reported that additional training in skills and strategies relevant to nontraditional combat operations would further reduce their stress and contribute to mission completion.

We did a side analysis of whether well-prepared individuals were less likely to report higher-than-usual work stress from frequently working long hours. Jex and Bliese (1999) found that self-efficacy beliefs moderate several factors that are positively related to stress: work overload, long work hours, and task significance. Although preparedness and self-efficacy are different concepts, we hypothesized that there was a positive correlation between preparation and beliefs about self-efficacy. Under this hypothesis, we expected that individuals who felt well prepared also felt more self-efficacious, and we estimated a model that interacted an indicator for "very well prepared" or "well prepared" with the variables for the number of times worked longer than the usual duty-day.[16]

Table 4.3
Predicted Probability of Higher-Than-Usual Work Stress, by Individual and Unit Preparedness

How well prepared?	Individual preparedness				Unit preparedness			
	Army	Navy	Marine Corps	Air Force	Army	Navy	Marine Corps	Air Force
Enlisted								
Very poorly	.43	.44	.31	.57	.52	.69	.41	.45
Poorly	.43	.50	.28	.43	.55	.60	.37	.52
Neither	.44	.49	.25	.41	.44	.49	.25	.41
Well	.40	.40	.18	.39	.42	.44	.30	.38
Very well	.34	.38	.15	.40	.40	.39	.27	.35
Officer								
Very poorly	.39	.27	.31	.39	.47	.64	.41	.29
Poorly	.33	.37	.28	.37	.39	.43	.37	.39
Neither	.27	.39	.25	.31	.27	.39	.25	.31
Well	.20	.32	.18	.34	.33	.39	.30	.31
Very well	.21	.30	.15	.35	.29	.31	.27	.26

NOTE: Predicted from regressions in Appendix B.

---

[16] At the same time, we dropped the interactions of "away" with the "worked" indicators. We also dropped the indicators for each level of individual preparedness—i.e., "very poorly," "poorly," "neither," "well," and "very well," replacing them with the single indicator for well prepared.

In most cases, the interactions were statistically insignificant as a set in the personal stress, work stress, and intention to stay regressions.[17] We visually inspected the coefficients on the interactions and found no support for the idea that the probability of higher-than-usual work stress increased less for well-prepared members than for non-well-prepared members. That is, we found no support for the finding of Jex and Bliese (1999). Again, this exploration was based on a hypothesis that preparation and belief of self-efficacy were positively correlated. Yet, the assumption may be false or the correlation may be weak: Perhaps our measure of individual preparedness is not a good surrogate for self-efficacy and a better measure would have supported their finding. Taking our result at face value, there was no significant interaction between individual preparedness and the number of times an individual worked longer than the usual duty-day, on higher-than-usual work stress, or on the intention to stay.

Higher-than-usual work stress was less likely for senior personnel, both enlisted and officer, than for junior personnel. A possible explanation is that senior personnel hold positions in which stressors occur less frequently, but that is improbable. More likely, stressors occur at similar rates, but senior personnel are more accustomed to anticipating and handling them. Also, senior officers have more control over working conditions. As Chapter Two noted, the literature on stress and performance finds that experience and training help people respond effectively to stressful situations. In addition, senior personnel are self-selected from junior personnel. Junior personnel who found service life stressful and had difficulty adapting to it might have left military service. The finding that stress is higher among junior service members is consistent with previous research conducted by the Walter Reed Institute (e.g., Campbell et al., 1998, Halverson et al., 1995).

Being Married Was Unrelated to Higher-Than-Usual Work Stress

The "married" coefficient is small and statistically insignificant in most of the work-stress regressions. However, "married" had a positive, usually significant, effect on the probability of higher-than-usual personal stress. Higher-than-usual personal stress was 3 to 4 percent more likely for married than for unmarried members. The results are consistent with the idea that stressors create similar work stress for married and single members but different personal stress. Work-related stressors may create family repercussions for married members, and family life produces stress of its own. The total amount of stress may, on average, be greater for a married member, and work- and family-generated stresses perhaps interact to amplify their effects.

The stress regressions also found that women were more likely than men to report higher-than-usual work stress, and whites were typically more likely than nonwhites to report higher-than-usual work stress. The finding that women report higher stress than men is consistent with the literature (Campbell et al., 1998; Halverson et al., 1995).

Intention to Stay

Similar factors determine higher-than-usual work stress and intention to stay, but have opposite effects. The factors include workload, whether time away was more or less than

---

[17] Results are available on request.

expected, and individual and unit preparedness. As a transition to the intention-to-stay regressions, we first consider the simple association between higher-than-usual work stress and intention to stay.

Higher-Than-Usual Work Stress and Intention to Stay

Service members who report higher-than-usual work stress also indicate a *higher* intention to stay on active duty. One might expect higher-than-usual work stress to be associated with lower intention to stay, but that is not the case. We found a positive association. That is, members who have a higher-than-usual level of work stress have a higher intention to stay on active duty. Figure 4.3 shows the percentage of members with higher-than-usual work stress with respect to their intention to stay, and Figure 4.4 shows the percentage of members with a positive intention to stay with respect to their level of work stress.[18] The patterns for personal stress are much the same.

The positive association is consistent with focus group discussions in that many participants intended to reenlist despite high levels of work stress, increased operational tempo, and long work hours. But we could not tell from these discussions whether reenlistment was likely to be higher among those with high stress than among those with low stress, whereas the positive association in the figures suggests that those with higher-than-usual work stress should have been more likely to state a positive intention to stay.

Figure 4.3
Higher-Than-Usual Work Stress, by Intention to Stay on Active Duty

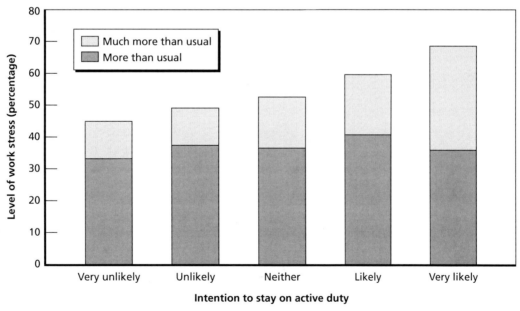

RAND *MG432-4.3*

---

[18] The figures are based on the overall sample; tabulations (not shown) by service, officer/enlisted, and junior showed similar patterns.

Figure 4.4
Positive Intention to Stay on Active Duty, by Level of Work Stress Relative to Individual's Usual Work Stress

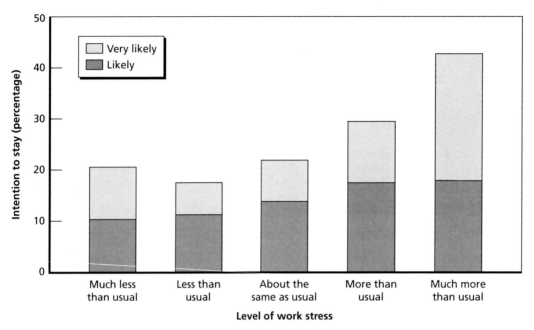

RAND *MG432-4.4*

The literature on this topic finds that moderate levels of stress lead to higher performance than either low or high levels of stress and, further, that moderate levels of stress induce increased group cooperation, commitment, and morale, thereby contributing to group effectiveness (Milgram, Orenstein, and Zafrir, 1989). In this context, an assignment in which a member perceives stress to be higher than usual may be providing stimulation and challenges that contribute to job satisfaction and the intention to stay. The mapping between the literature and our finding is somewhat ambiguous, however, because studies in the literature employ specific stressors and vary the level of the stressor, whereas the survey respondents are asked to report how their level of stress compares with their "usual" level of stress—however they wish to interpret that level. We do not know how the respondent's perception of "higher-than-usual" work stress maps into studies that vary a specific stressor from low to moderate to high levels.

We suggest an alternative explanation for the positive association between higher-than-usual work stress and intention to stay—an internal sorting process whereby personnel with a good match to the military are assigned to positions that more frequently have episodes of higher stress. Such personnel may have a positive intention to stay and be more capable of handling stress. Also, as the literature suggests, the stress might contribute to their intention to stay, provided the stress is "moderate."[19] However, we found that, throughout its range, frequently working longer than the usual duty-day causes an increase in the probability of higher-than-usual work stress and a decrease in the probability of intention to stay (see below). The uniformly negative relationship between this stressor and intention to stay

---

[19] Studies find that retention intentions are a good predictor of actual retention (e.g., Rakoff, Griffith, and Zarkin, 1994), but such work has not focused on the effect of stress on intention and subsequent retention.

raises doubt that the positive effect of moderate stress on performance is a dominant factor in the positive association between higher-than-usual work stress and intention to stay. If it were, we might expect an inverted U-shaped relationship, with intention to stay at first increasing and then decreasing as the frequency of working long days increased.

Figure 4.4 also shows a slight upturn in the intention to continue if work stress is much less than usual. This too is consistent with sorting. Perhaps members who prefer low-stress positions are assigned to them, and some of those positions persistently have stress that is much lower than usual. Similarly, members who like the military but cannot handle high-stress positions may be repeatedly assigned to low-stress positions. The same upturn occurs, only more prominently, when intention is plotted against personal stress.

Overview of Regression on Intentions

We ran linear probability models for four indicators of intentions:

- Intention to stay on active duty
- Intention to stay on active duty for 20 years
- Whether being away last year, or lack thereof, increased your desire to stay
- Whether your spouse or significant other thinks you should stay on active duty.[20]

The explanatory variables in each regression include indicators for the number of times the member worked longer than the usual duty-day in the past 12 months, whether the member was away from his/her permanent duty station in the past 12 months, the interactions between worked longer and away, whether the member reported being involved in combat operations in OEF/OIF, indicators for whether time away was less than or greater than expected, indicators for individual preparedness and unit preparedness, and indicators for senior, married, female, and nonwhite. The indicators are based on the member's response—i.e., the member's perception of the unit's preparedness for its wartime mission.

We begin with a qualitative summary of the results. Tables 4.4 and 4.5 provide a guide to the statistical significance of F-tests for sets of variables and t-tests for particular indicators within the sets, for enlisted and officers.[21] The main lesson is that, of the four intention regressions, the regression on intention to stay has the largest number of significant explanatory variables and in that sense fits the data best.

---

[20] We also ran regressions on two other variables but do not report their results: an indicator for total expected years of service and an indicator for whether the member's family wanted him or her to stay on active duty. The indicator for total expected years of service took four values ("1" for 5 or fewer years of service, "2" for 6–9, "3" for 10–19, and "4" for 20 or more) and was available only in the March 2003 survey. Because there was no variable in the public-use data for years of service, we could not control for how many years the member had already served. The results were qualitatively similar to those for the intention to stay in service. The indicator for whether the family wanted the member to stay on active duty was available only for the July 2003 survey. It was not clear whether "family" referred to immediate family—i.e., spouse and children—or to parents, siblings, and relatives, or both. The regression had low explanatory power, and the findings were similar to, but statistically weaker than, the results for the regression on whether the member's spouse or significant other wanted the member to stay.

[21] For pairings such as "worked long 61–120 times" and "worked long more than 120 times," or "very well/well prepared," the table reflects the higher of their t-tests.

Table 4.4
Statistical Significance of Variables in Intention Regressions for Enlisted Members

Variables	Stay				Stay 20				Increase stay				Spouse stay			
	Army	Navy	Marine Corps	Air Force	Army	Navy	Marine Corps	Air Force	Army	Navy	Marine Corps	Air Force	Army	Navy	Marine Corps	Air Force
Worked longer than usual day																
Worked long >60 times																
Away*worked longer																
Combat OEF/OIF					*	*	*	*								
Time away vs. expected time away																
Much less than/less than																
Much more than/more than																
Are you prepared?																
Very poorly/poorly prepared																
Very well/well prepared																
Unit prepared?																
Very poorly/poorly prepared																
Very well/well prepared																
Senior																
Married																
Female																
Nonwhite																

Significance levels: Not significant   0.10   0.05   0.01   * Not available

SOURCE: Authors' regressions and F-tests.
RAND MG432-Tab 4.4

Table 4.5
Statistical Significance of Variables in Intention Regressions for Officers

Variables	Stay				Stay 20				Increase stay				Spouse stay			
	Army	Navy	Marine Corps	Air Force	Army	Navy	Marine Corps	Air Force	Army	Navy	Marine Corps	Air Force	Army	Navy	Marine Corps	Air Force
Worked longer than usual day																
Worked long >60 times																
Away*worked longer																
Combat OEF/OIF					*	*	*	*								
Time away vs. expected time away																
Much less than/less than																
Much more than/more than																
Are you prepared?																
Very poorly/poorly prepared																
Very well/well prepared																
Unit prepared?																
Very poorly/poorly prepared																
Very well/well prepared																
Senior																
Married																
Female																
Nonwhite																

Significance levels: ☐ Not significant ▨ 0.10 ▨ 0.05 ■ 0.01 * Not available

SOURCE: Authors' regressions and F-tests.

RAND MG432-Tab 4.5

Intention to Stay on Active Duty

Table 4.6 shows the mirrorlike similarity of the explanatory variable effects in the work-stress and intention-to-stay regressions. Variables significant in the work-stress regression are often significant in the intention-to-stay regression. The significant variables include the number of times worked longer than the usual duty-day, whether time away was more or less than expected, individual preparedness, and unit preparedness. Combat was usually not significant, and the interactions between "away" and "worked longer" were usually not significant.

The significant variables usually worked in opposite directions:

- The probability of higher-than-usual work stress was higher and the probability of intention to stay was lower when the member very frequently worked longer than the usual duty-day and was away much longer than expected.

Table 4.6
Statistical Significance of Selected Variables in Higher-Than-Usual Work Stress and Intention-to-Stay Regressions

Variable	Higher-than-usual work stress				Intention to stay			
	A	N	M	A	A	N	M	A
Enlisted								
Worked long†	***	***	***	***	**	***	***	***
61–120 times	***	***	***	***	*	***	***	*
>120 times	***	***	***	***	***	**		***
Away*worked long†		**				*	**	
61–120 times		**						
>120 times							**	
Combat				*	*			
Time away†	***	***		***		***		***
Much more than expected	***	***		***	**	***		***
Individual preparedness†	***	**			***	***	**	***
Very well prepared	***	***	*		***	***	***	***
Unit preparedness†	***	***	***	***	***	***	**	***
Very well prepared		***	**	**	***	*	**	***
Officer								
Worked long†	***	***	***	***	***			*
61–120 times	***	***	***	***	***			**
>120 times	***	***	***	***	***		**	*
Away*worked long†			**					
61–120 times								
>120 times								
Combat	*		**		***			
Time away†	***	**	***	***	***	***		***
Much more than expected	***	***	**	***	***	***	**	***
Individual preparedness†					***		***	**
Very well prepared		**	**		**		***	*
Unit preparedness†	**	***			***	***	***	**
Very well prepared		*			***	***	***	**

SOURCE: Tests on regressions in Appendix B.
Key: A, N, M, A = Army, Navy, Marine Corps, Air Force.
† = a set of indicator variables.
Significance levels: *** = .01;   ** = .05;   * = .10;   ☐ = not significant.

- The probability of higher-than-usual work stress was lower and the probability of intention to stay was higher when the member felt very well prepared to do his or her wartime job and felt that the unit was very well prepared for its wartime mission.

Officers differed from enlisted members somewhat. Individual preparedness and unit preparedness were not as significant in mitigating work stress for officers, and working long days was often not significant in the intention equation, perhaps because officers routinely expect to work long days.

The finding that many of the variables work in opposite directions seems intuitive, but at the same time seems to conflict with the positive simple relationship between stress and intention discussed above. The conflict can be resolved by recognizing that the effects of the factors in the regression do not dominate the simple relationship. For instance, an increase in the number of times worked longer than the usual duty-day increases the probability of higher-than-usual work stress and reduces the probability of intention to stay, but not by enough to overcome the positive relationship between stress and intention. If the regression effects dominated, stress and intention would be negatively correlated because variables that decreased intention would also increase higher-than-usual stress.

Higher Frequency of Working Longer-Than-Usual Duty-Day Reduced Intention to Stay on Active Duty, and This Effect Did Not Differ Between Those Who Were and Were Not Away from Home in the Past Year

The regression results for intention to stay showed that frequently working longer than the usual duty-day reduced the intention to stay on active duty (Table 4.7). This result is consistent with previous literature on this topic, which finds that work hours are reported by a large number of personnel as a reason to leave the military (Huffman et al., 2001a, b) and

Table 4.7
Predicted Probability of Intention to Stay, by Worked Longer and Whether Away from Permanent Duty Station in Past Year

Times worked longer than usual duty-day	Army		Navy		Marine Corps		Air Force	
	Not away	Away	Not away	Away	Not away	Away	Not away	Away
Enlisted								
0–20	.36	.37	.33	.30	.29	.27	.41	.39
21–60	.34	.26	.31	.26	.23	.17	.36	.36
61–120	.30	.28	.21	.26	.15	.17	.34	.34
>120	.27	.24	.25	.30	.28	.12	.31	.32
Officer								
0–20	.62	.57	.53	.60	.55	.55	.54	.37
21–60	.54	.60	.54	.52	.48	.47	.55	.53
61–120	.48	.55	.54	.54	.50	.44	.58	.58
>120	.50	.50	.53	.56	.47	.45	.66	.58

SOURCE: Predicted from regressions in Appendix B.

is supported by focus group discussions. Some focus group participants reported that long work hours were causing them to consider leaving or decide to leave the military. The result is also consistent with the model in Chapter Two, in that frequently working long duty-days can be expected to reduce the satisfaction from military activities, and therefore reduce the intention to stay.

There was practically no difference in the effect of the number of times worked longer than the usual duty-day on the intention to stay between members who were, or were not, away from their permanent duty stations in the past year. The set of coefficients for the interactions between "away" and "worked longer" were not significant, except for Navy and Marine Corps enlisted personnel, and in their case the effect on intention was small.

In the Period Circa Mid-2002 to Mid-2003, Being in Combat Operations in OEF/OIF Had No Effect on the Intention to Stay in the Navy, Marine Corps, or Air Force, but It Reduced Intention in the Army

In the Army, intention to stay decreased by 0.07 for enlisted and 0.12 for officers (see coefficients of the combat variable in Appendix B, Tables B.5 and B.6). As discussed in Chapter Two, previous studies found that hostile deployments in the 1990s had little effect on reenlistment (Hosek and Totten, 2002; Fricker, 2002). Our Army results are therefore likely to differ from previous work, assuming soldiers act on their intentions. Also, ground conditions in Iraq have become increasingly hostile since mid-2003 as the insurgency has grown and its tactics have become more sophisticated and lethal. As a result, the combat findings in our data may not be a useful guide to more-recent experience.

Longer Time Away Relative to Expected Time Away Decreased Intention to Stay

The results consistently showed that if time away was much more than expected, the intention to stay was lower (Table 4.8). Also, in most but not all cases, if time away was less than expected, the intention to stay was slightly higher than if actual time equaled expected time. This is consistent with Hosek and Totten (2002), who found that reenlistment declined as the duration of deployment extended beyond the average duration of deployment, as well as with focus group comments on the negative effect of deployment uncertainty on morale. Further, it is consistent with the model presented in Chapter Two.

The model implies that the individual would prefer to know the exact length of the deployment rather than be subject to a random length. Even if an exact length cannot credibly be given, the model implies that the individual would prefer to know that the deployment will be, say, 12 months long plus or minus a month, rather than a random length centered at 12 months plus or minus two months. One might alternatively conjecture that many people prefer uncertainty because it better matches their preference for deployment when and only when an important job needs to be done.[22] If so, knowing in advance might remove some sense of deployment for a purpose. But the model implies that service members, although dedicated, would not necessarily be willing to deploy for "as long as it takes." Even if they are willing to deploy for a long period, the model implies that they would prefer a certain to an uncertain length of deployment.

---

[22] We thank Gail Zellman for suggesting this point.

Table 4.8
Predicted Probability of Intention to Stay on Active Duty,
by Whether Time Away Was Less or More Than Expected

Time away relative to expected time away	Army	Navy	Marine Corps	Air Force
Enlisted				
Much less	.34	.32	.28	.44
Less	.39	.33	.27	.40
Neither	.36	.33	.29	.41
More	.36	.27	.27	.38
Much more	.31	.17	.27	.24
Officer				
Much less	.60	.50	.54	.59
Less	.57	.58	.54	.59
Neither	.62	.53	.55	.58
More	.58	.54	.53	.49
Much more	.48	.38	.46	.44

SOURCE: Predicted from regressions in Appendix B.

The survey analysis provides a simple test of this preference for certainty. Under the alternative, if service members thought they were deployed for an important purpose, they would be indifferent to whether the deployment was longer or shorter than expected. The analysis rejects this alternative; being away for longer than expected reduces intention to stay. The result is consistent with the model and suggests that, although service members may embrace the purpose of deployment, they also have preferences for more certainty over the mix of their time between deployment and home.

Individual Preparedness Increased Intention to Stay

Individuals who felt very well prepared for their wartime jobs had a higher intention to stay (Table 4.9). This also tended to be true of individuals who felt well prepared. Many members fall into these two categories. About 30 to 40 percent described themselves as very well prepared, and 42 to 50 percent described themselves as well prepared.[23] Enlisted members who felt very poorly prepared had a lower intention to stay; this finding was significant for enlisted members but not for officers, but it was based on quite small numbers: Only 1 to 3 percent of enlisted members and 0 to 2 percent of officers described themselves as very poorly prepared.

[23] See Defense Manpower Data Center, March 2003 Status of Forces Survey of Active-Duty Members: Tabulations of Responses (2003a); and Defense Manpower Data Center, July 2003 Status of Forces Survey of Active-Duty Members: Tabulations of Responses (2003b).

Table 4.9
Predicted Probability of Intention to Stay on Active Duty, by Individual and Unit Preparedness

How well prepared?	Individual preparedness				Unit preparedness			
	Army	Navy	Marine Corps	Air Force	Army	Navy	Marine Corps	Air Force
Enlisted								
Very poorly	.28	.19	.22	.25	.27	.30	.16	.24
Poorly	.36	.35	.29	.43	.34	.19	.27	.32
Neither	.36	.33	.29	.41	.36	.33	.29	.41
Well	.42	.45	.37	.48	.42	.33	.31	.47
Very well	.45	.50	.40	.51	.44	.38	.36	.49
Officer								
Very poorly	.42	.53	.34	.54	.53	.26	.41	.37
Poorly	.51	.50	.44	.55	.53	.37	.45	.53
Neither	.62	.53	.55	.58	.62	.53	.55	.58
Well	.70	.58	.66	.66	.65	.62	.64	.58
Very well	.70	.55	.66	.66	.72	.64	.67	.66

SOURCE: Predicted from regressions in Appendix B.

Similarly, Unit Preparedness Increased Intention to Stay

Members who felt that their unit was very well prepared or well prepared had a higher intention to stay, while those who felt that their unit was very poorly prepared or poorly prepared had a lower intention to stay (Table 4.9). About 18 to 30 percent and 39 to 52 percent thought their unit was very well prepared or well prepared, respectively, and only 1 to 2 percent thought that their unit was very poorly prepared, except for Army enlisted, for whom the figure was 6 percent. The relevance of preparation to reenlistment intentions corresponds closely to the importance that focus group participants placed on effective training as a means of reducing their work stress and improving their ability to successfully complete their missions.

We also found that senior members had a higher intention to stay than did junior members, and married members had a higher intention to stay than did unmarried members. Part of this difference reflects selective retention: People enter military service at junior ranks, and senior members consist of entrants who chose to remain in military service. Also, most members enter the military unmarried and tend to marry in service if they find the military lifestyle suitable.

We next briefly discuss the results for regressions on the other indicators of the intention to stay on active duty and then conclude the chapter.

Intention to Stay for 20 Years[24]

We were surprised to find that intention to stay for 20 years was not, in most cases, significantly affected by the frequency of times worked longer than duty-day.[25] This finding suggests that current work circumstances are not a major factor in the member's career decision. Still, this finding is consistent with the expected-utility model. The model implies that expected utility is independent of a current outcome of deployment; however, if the current deployment causes the member to change his or her expectation of future deployment, then future expected utility will also change. The same type of reasoning implies that the current frequency of working longer than the usual duty-day might be entirely consistent with the member's expectations, and the member has no reason to change the future expectation of working longer than the usual duty-day; hence, there is no change in expected utility or intention to stay.

Being away less time, or more time, than expected had mixed effects. It decreased intention to stay for 20 years for soldiers and sailors, particularly if they were away much more than expected, but did not matter for Marines and airmen. Intention to stay for 20 years was higher for members who felt that they and their units were well prepared. Unit preparation also mattered, particularly if the unit was perceived as being poorly prepared, which, as mentioned, was rare. The results for officers pointed to the importance of individual preparedness, as they did for enlisted members. Unit preparation seemed to be less important than it was in the intention-to-stay regression, however. Perhaps this difference is because officers expected to be reassigned to different units as their careers progressed, implying that their current units' preparedness was not particularly relevant to a career decision.

Did Being Away Last Year, or the Lack Thereof, Increase Your Desire to Stay?

This question was asked of all respondents. The desire to stay might have been affected by being away or by *not* being away ("lack thereof"). This dependent variable reflects a change in intentions, whereas the other intention variables reflect a level of intention. The regressions on "increased your desire to stay" have lower explanatory power (R-squared) and fewer significant coefficients than the regressions for intention to stay and intention to stay for 20 years.

Frequently working longer than the usual duty-day reduced the desire to stay, although the decrease was fairly small: Serving in combat operations in OEF/OIF decreased a soldier's intention to stay by −0.03 and increased a Marine's intention by 0.06. The combat indicator was not significant for sailors or airmen or for officers in any service. Time away that was less or much less than expected increased the desire to stay, and this variable was significant for enlisted members in every service. Time away that was more than expected tended to decrease the desire to stay. Also, the desire to stay increased if enlisted members felt that they and their unit were very well or well prepared. An exception was sailors' increased desire to stay if they felt poorly prepared and felt their unit was poorly prepared—an anomalous finding that might simply reflect sailors who had returned from a deployment in

---

[24] We could only estimate a regression on the intention to stay for 20 years with the July 2003 survey, so the sample size was about half of that for the regression on intention to stay, which was based on March and July 2003 surveys (Defense Manpower Data Center, 2003a, b).

[25] These variables were significant only for sailors, and in their case the pattern of coefficients can be interpreted as saying that sailors who never worked longer than the usual duty-day were about 0.13 more likely to stay for 20 years than the many sailors who worked one or more times longer than the usual duty-day.

high spirits but whose ship needed refitting for the next deployment. Officers in the four services had similar, although weaker, relationships to those of enlisted members.

Interestingly, we found that members with the highest intention to stay were more likely to report the greatest decrease in their desire to stay, and that members with a higher intention to stay also tended to report higher-than-usual work stress. We suggested that the positive association between stress and intention reflected sorting. If positions of responsibility are prone to episodes of higher-than-usual stress—e.g., from frequently working longer than the usual duty-day—then members with a higher intention to stay might be expected to have a greater decrease in intention. That is what we find in Figure 4.5. Nearly half of those very likely to stay on active duty said their desire to stay had decreased or greatly decreased, whereas fewer than 10 percent of those very unlikely to stay reported any decrease. The distribution of members by intention is as follows: very likely, 13 percent; likely, 14 percent; neither likely nor unlikely, 14 percent; unlikely, 29 percent; very unlikely, 31 percent.

Spouse/Significant Other Thinks You Should Stay on Active Duty

This variable reflects the member's perception of whether his or her spouse or significant other thought the member should stay on active duty. This perception was less likely when the member had often worked longer than the usual duty-day or had been away longer than expected. A high frequency of working longer than the usual duty-day had a negative effect for enlisted members and for Army officers, but not for officers in other services. Time away

Figure 4.5
Percentage of Members with "Decreased" or "Greatly Decreased" Desire to Stay, by Level of Intention to Stay on Active Duty

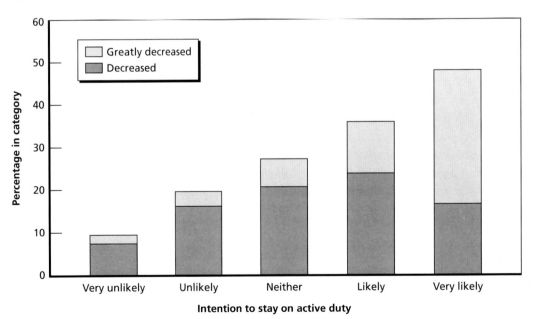

being more than expected had a negative effect for sailors and airmen, and for officers across the board. Considering that time away from home by the service member places additional burden on the spouse or significant other, especially if children are involved, this result should be expected. It is consistent with the model and the focus groups, wherein some service members said that their spouses became less supportive of military service as deployments became more frequent and longer.

Individual and unit preparedness were by and large significant factors for enlisted members and officers; members who felt well prepared (poorly prepared) were more likely to indicate that their spouse or significant other wanted them (did not want them) to stay on active duty. Previous research supports the strong effect of spousal support for a military career on reenlistment intentions of service members (Mohr, Holzbach, and Morrison, 1981; Orthner, 1980; Kirby and Naftel, 1998). Rosen and Durand (1995) found that spousal support is one of the most significant predictors of retention behavior for both NCOs and junior enlisted personnel.

Summary

Our quantitative findings have suggested several important relationships that relate to the model in Chapter Two, are consistent with the literature, and offer a basis for our focus group observations.

First, the stress regressions show that the number of times worked longer than normal duty-day, not time spent away from home base, is what drives the reported stress of individuals. This is true of higher-than-usual work stress, which was the focus of our discussion above, and also true of higher-than-usual personal stress. In other words, being away, on its own, does not seem to increase the perceived work stress of personnel. Only to the extent that individuals must work longer hours more frequently on deployment does being away actually factor into the work stress of service members.

This finding is somewhat surprising, because one would expect that being in a strange place with potentially poor living conditions, away from one's family, and possibly in personal danger, would increase stress above and beyond that caused by long work hours. But that was not the case in the period covered by our survey samples: mid-2002 to mid-2003. We did hear in focus groups that the conditions on deployments were often less stressful, because service members could focus on their jobs and did not have to attend to the other administrative and training tasks that they did on base.

Another significant finding is that higher-than-usual work stress is more likely when a service member's time away from home is more or much more than expected. The model in Chapter Two implies that a member prefers certainty in the amount of deployment time, and time away that is far longer than expected suggests considerable uncertainty. This result also corresponds to our focus group discussions. Members were frustrated as deployment leave and return times changed. Individual and unit preparedness were significant in reducing the likelihood of higher-than-usual work stress.

We explored whether individual preparedness interacted with the number of times an individual worked longer than the usual duty-day. This data experiment was motivated by a finding in the literature that high self-efficacy moderated the effect of a high workload on producing psychological strain, compared with low self-efficacy. However, using an assumption that high individual preparedness was positively correlated with self-efficacy, we found no support for the hypothesis that service members who felt well or very well prepared were less likely to have higher-than-usual work stress as the number of times they worked longer than the usual duty-day increased, compared with other service members.

Finally, as suggested in the literature on this topic, we found that higher-than-usual work stress was less likely for more senior personnel (E-5–E-9, O-4–O-6). Several explanations were offered for these differences, including the fact, mentioned frequently in the literature on this topic, that the additional training and experience of senior personnel are likely to help them deal more effectively with stress.

We found a simple positive association between higher-than-usual work stress and intention to stay: Members who report higher-than-usual levels of work stress also report higher intentions to stay on active duty. We think this association reflects an internal sorting mechanism whereby individuals who are well matched to the military are more likely to be placed in positions involving more-frequent stress and are more capable of handling that stress. However, we also found, via regression, that explanatory variables typically had opposite effects on higher-than-usual work stress and intention to stay. Frequently working longer than the usual duty-day, for instance, increased the probability of higher-than-usual stress and the probability of decreased intention to stay, outcomes that would suggest a negative relationship between higher-than-usual stress and intention. Yet, the effects found in the regressions were not strong enough to overturn the positive association between higher-than-usual stress and intention. Consistent with this positive association, service members with whom we spoke in the focus groups did not report that additional job stress as a result of increased work tempo would cause them to leave the military.

As noted, the variables in the regressions generally worked in opposite directions on regressions of higher-than-usual work stress and decreased the probability of intention to stay. Perhaps both regressions express a single underlying factor reflecting willingness to stay. The effect of an explanatory variable that increased the factor would be observed by higher intention to stay and lower-than-usual work stress. That is, the self-reported level of stress would not be stress per se but a measure of willingness to stay. A mimic model could potentially estimate the underlying factor.[26] Whatever the interpretation, the underlying factor would be of policy importance if it proved to be a better predictor of subsequent continuation in the military than the intention-to-stay variable, which is customarily used. The underlying factor could be validated empirically with data on intentions linked to data on subsequent choices to stay or leave.

Finally, it is worth keeping in mind that our data and the experiences discussed in the focus groups came from a period early in OEF/OIF. The retrospective period for the surveys was mid-2002 to mid-2003, and the focus groups were held in early 2004. During 2004 and 2005, the insurgency in Iraq became far more active and lethal, some U.S. personnel were ordered to continue on duty under "stop-loss provisions,"[27] and increasing numbers of

---

[26] In a mimic model, the outcomes stress and intention to stay would be modeled as a function of the underlying factor and an error term, and the underlying factor would depend on the explanatory variables we have used and an unobserved person-specific factor. See, for example, Jöreskog and Goldberger (1975).

[27] A *stop-loss provision* compels a service member to remain on duty even though he or she has reached the end of his/her term of service.

personnel faced their second or even third deployment. It remains to be seen how these changes might alter the findings in our research.

CHAPTER FIVE

Conclusions

The findings and observations discussed in this monograph demonstrate that the effect of deployments on military personnel, their attitudes toward the military, and their reenlistment intentions must be considered in a multidimensional framework. Deployments not only have different, and even conflicting, effects across individuals, but also affect the same individual service member in multiple ways. Discussions with service members and analysis of survey data suggest that individuals have varying attitudes toward military life and find that military life includes aspects that are rewarding and challenging, as well as those that are frustrating and demoralizing. It is worth noting, however, that findings in this monograph suggest a high degree of resiliency and effectiveness among military personnel across all services in the face of many different challenges.

Positive Aspects of Deployment

Service members appreciate deployments as an opportunity to participate in meaningful missions. It goes without saying that missions should be meaningful from a military perspective; in addition, they should be clearly defined and perceived as meaningful by service members. For military planners, deployments and rotation cycles should be designed to be inclusive, allowing all qualified personnel an opportunity to use their skills and contribute to the central objective, rather than concentrating deployments on a subset of the force.

In general, service members in our focus group reported more positive feelings toward deployments and were more willing to tolerate the negative aspects of deployment when they were doing work that seemed necessary and important. In fact, the opportunity to use one's training and skills in a real-world situation was one of the reasons that some personnel with whom we spoke preferred deployments to time spent at home base, or at least looked forward to deployment. At the same time, service members, particularly the most junior service members in our groups, appeared to feel that much of the work done on the base was unnecessary or not the type of work they joined the service to do, and some of them resented being forced to work long hours for no real purpose. These focus group observations offer a possible explanation of why in our data analysis the deployment indicator was not significantly related to intention to stay. Deployment, although arduous and demanding, was meaningful and satisfying, whereas nondeployment also could be demanding but was not always meaningful.

This finding suggests that the military should work hard to define and communicate both an overarching mission and how daily tasks contribute to that mission. For many personnel, deployments present an opportunity to achieve something extraordinary, to overcome obstacles and challenges, and to develop close bonds with unit members. Many service members reported that they were proud of what they had accomplished on their deployments. Returning service members were also proud of the respect they received from civilians and other people who looked up to them because of their accomplishments in the military. These sentiments were likely to contribute to overall positive attitudes toward deployment.

However, these benefits seem to have lost some of their luster for service members who had been deployed multiple times in their career. Some of these personnel had grown tired of long, difficult deployments and were dismayed by the prospect of repeated, long separations from their family in the future.

Deployment Pay

Deployment pay helped to offset some of the negative aspects of deployment. Military officials should reconsider, and are reconsidering, additional ways to compensate personnel who are sent on unusually long, frequent, or arduous deployments.

Deployment pay is another significant positive aspect of deployments, one that even motivates personnel to volunteer for difficult duty. Personnel not only receive special pays and tax exemptions for their deployments, but they also have fewer opportunities to spend their money (especially true for single personnel). The result is that many return home with a significant amount of savings, a reward for their sacrifice.

The effect of deployment pay on reenlistment and service member attitudes toward the military is documented in previous research and is also something that we heard about in our focus groups. Service members report using extra money to pay off loans or credit-card debt, to save for college, or to buy such items as cars. In this way, the rewards of a hard deployment can have long-term effects for military personnel. Deployment pay is also one benefit of deployment that can be shared by the entire family and helps to compensate families for long separations, including absences from such major events as the birth of a child, birthdays, holiday gatherings, or the illness or injury of a loved one. Deployment pay also helps to offset the additional work, harsh living conditions, and risk that come with deployment.

The model in Chapter Two implies that, as deployment time extends beyond the level a service member prefers, utility declines at an increasing rate. For some, the decrease in utility may be enough to deter the service member from making the military a career or even continuing beyond the current term or obligation. Because long deployment causes a nonlinear decrease in utility, the model implies that deployment pay should increase nonlinearly to offset this decrease. The model discussion notes that the relationship between deployment length and utility also depends on the conditions of the deployment—for example, how dangerous and arduous it is—the idea being that utility in long deployments will decrease more rapidly in worse conditions.

Although current deployment pays point in the direction of this flexibility, the services and the Office of the Secretary of Defense recognize the need to restructure deployment pay. High Deployment Pay, a pay enacted before September 11, 2001, provides $100 per day for members deployed over the predefined threshold of 400 days in any 730-day period or more than 191 days in a 365-day period. But this pay was, in effect, a disciplining device to prevent the services from deploying personnel extensively, and, in an era of war on terrorism, it is widely seen as over-restrictive because it does not allow the services the flexibility to deploy personnel for as long or as frequently as they are needed to meet military requirements, without incurring extremely large expense. This pay has therefore been suspended. Another deployment pay is "Hardship Duty Pay for Involuntary Extension of Duty," which pays $100 per month for members assigned or attached to specific units in the Iraqi area of operations who have been in Iraq and/or Afghanistan for 12 months within a 15-month period and have been asked to stay past the 12-month rotation date. However, the most common deployment pays—Family Separation and Hostile Duty Pays—pay a flat rate per month (currently $250 per month for Family Separation Pay and $225 per month for Hostile Duty Pay).

Consistent with our analysis that deployment pay should increase nonlinearly with the duration and danger/arduousness of a deployment, and yet acting on their own assessment of the situation, the services and OSD are working together to reformulate deployment pay. In particular, they are considering using the statutory authority under Hardship Duty Pay to create "tempo-based" deployment pay, which takes into account the duration, frequency, and conditions (arduousness) of deployment, and, where the pay rates may vary from service to service, depending on the conditions of deployment, the needs to sustain retention and morale, and the presence of other pays (e.g., Sea Pay in the Navy). In addition, the Army is considering "warrior pay," which, as with Sea Pay, would be a permanent supplement to basic pay for the soldiers, depending on their cumulative amount of deployment.

These changes are responsive not only to incumbent personnel but also to prospective recruits. If prospective recruits now anticipate more-frequent, long, dangerous deployments than in the past, our model and analysis suggest that they will demand higher pay to compensate for placing themselves at greater risk. It remains to be determined whether the higher pay should be in the form of higher deployment pay, higher basic pay (or enlistment incentives), or both. These are topics requiring further study, and we offer no specific recommendations here. We note, however, that the difficulty in Army recruiting in 2005 in the actives, Reserves, and National Guard is consistent with the notion that prospective recruits are deterred by the greater risk and burden of deployment, and that the greater availability and level of enlistment bonuses have been an appropriate countermeasure. Also, reenlistment bonuses, Hazardous Duty Pay, Family Separation Pay, and Sea Pay, and the nontaxability of military pay for members serving in a combat zone have increased deployment-related pay, thereby helping to sustain retention.

Addressing Negative Aspects of Deployment

Family separation, high operational tempo, long work hours, and uncertainty are cited as the most significant negative aspects of deployment and are shown in data analysis to affect reenlistment intentions and work stress. To address concerns about work hours and operational tempo, attention should be paid to the hours worked by military personnel and efforts should be made to distribute work and deployments where possible. To reduce uncertainty, communication between military leaders and service members should be as frequent and accurate as security circumstances permit.

Finally, analysis is required to determine how to decrease family-separation stress—for example, through the use of additional family-support programs, pre- and postdeployment briefings and counseling for the member and spouse, better communication home for deployed personnel, and even small travel awards for spouses who want to move back home when the member is deployed.

Family Separation

Of the reported negative features of deployment, separation from family was probably the most significant complaint that we heard from focus group members, especially those who deploy, and one of the most frequently given explanations by those planning to leave the service. Data analysis showing the effect of spousal attitudes toward military service supports the idea that family separation affects the reenlistment intentions of personnel. Service members with whom we spoke said that being away from their spouses and children is hard on their relationships and hard on them emotionally. Service members reported that separation associated with deployment does not really begin at the time that they leave home, but well before, in the predeployment phase. Predeployment preparations and training exercises often take personnel away from their families and disrupt their lives substantially. Once deployed, communication home was reported as a frequent problem. Phones were few, unreliable, often broken, and very expensive. Email was also unreliable and difficult to access, given the ratio of computers to personnel. Installing better methods of communication would seem to be one easy way to improve the quality of life for personnel on long, exhausting deployments.

Reintegrating into the family unit upon returning home is another challenge. If frequent, long deployments continue to be common, additional and more-developed family support systems may be needed. Family-support programs could be used to keep family members informed about the status of the deployment, help spouses to deal with unforeseen problems, and offer counseling to spouses and children. Service members are also likely to be more willing to deploy and more able to focus on their jobs while on deployment if they feel that their families are being taken care of at home. Many family-support programs already exist throughout the service, but there has not been an extended study of their effectiveness, rates of use, and cost-effectiveness in a period of high operational tempo. Such a study would seem to be an area for future work. A longitudinal or unit-based study could help to identify the strengths and weaknesses of existing support programs and to target areas for improvement. Attention should also be given to the best way to serve families living off-base who might find it inconvenient to use on-base family support and who might prefer money instead of such services—for example, money for childcare.

Finally, we learned from our focus groups that some military spouses of deployed personnel return to their hometowns during the deployment, often to live with their families. This is an alternative support structure. Little is known about how often this return home occurs, whether it disrupts the cohesion of the military community on-base, whether it is beneficial to the well-being of the spouse, and whether it prevents marital problems. The spouses who return to their hometowns do not use on-base facilities, and it may be worth considering whether to give them a small award to cover the cost of their travel.

Operational Tempo and Work Hours

Some service members cited the number and frequency of deployments as a negative aspect of military life. Deployments are not unexpected for military personnel. From discussions with military personnel in all services, Marines seemed to expect the most deployment, whereas Army personnel expected to deploy but were still surprised by back-to-back deployments. Navy and Air Force personnel also expected to deploy, particularly Navy personnel in seagoing ratings (occupational areas).

Importantly, there appears to be a good deal of self-selection into service branch and occupational area—that is, those in the Air Force joined the Air Force and not a different service because they did not want to deploy many times and did not want to participate in ground combat, which they expected would be the case if they joined the Marines or Army. Selection into occupations also occurs when individuals who want to deploy tend to choose occupations that include more time deployed. However, despite the fact that most expected to deploy, some members with whom we spoke—both junior and career personnel—were still surprised at the length and frequency of current deployments, and some felt that the pace of deployment, if continued into the future, would make it difficult to maintain a balance between their family life and their commitment to military service. Steps to spread the burden of deployments and compensate those who have been on back-to-back deployments would be useful for addressing these concerns.

Another important finding that emerges from this monograph is that high operational tempo and long work hours are aspects of military life that affect all personnel, deployed and nondeployed. The analysis of Status of Forces surveys presented in this monograph shows that frequently working longer than the usual duty-day increases the likelihood of higher-than-usual work stress and personal stress, and decreases the intention to stay. Without a doubt, personnel who are deployed work long days more frequently, but nondeployed personnel often must put in 60- to 80-hour weeks as well. These findings were confirmed by focus group discussions.

Given the stress that long work hours place on personnel, military planners should continually review why personnel must work longer than the normal duty-day so frequently, whether certain tasks can be eliminated or postponed, and whether personnel can be reallocated from other assignments on-base or from one base to another in order to spread the burden of work more effectively. Also, unlike deployed personnel, nondeployed personnel receive no additional pay, even though they may work unusually long days to support deployments. A special "long hours" pay for these personnel may be worth considering. The pay would be intended to recognize the extraordinary effort required to support operations.

Uncertainty

Communication between the military and the service member is another area of concern for military personnel. Service members in our focus groups complained about the ambiguity of deployments, in terms of start and/or end date and nature of the mission. Personnel with whom we spoke would like to be given more clarity about when they will leave and return and what they will do, and they expect honesty and openness about the demands that will be placed on them. This finding is consistent with previous literature and with the model in Chapter Two. Personnel tend to report more-positive attitudes toward deployments, both hypothetically and retrospectively, when they are able to form accurate, or realistic, expectations about their deployment conditions, duties, and length. Less ambiguity and frequent communication would help service members develop realistic expectations and could also boost individual and unit morale.

Effective means of communication would help to alleviate the strains coming from uncertainty about the date of return from a deployment. There are limits to what can be done, however: Military commanders must have the flexibility to change tour lengths and rotation cycles in response to emergent needs in an operation. Stabilizing deployment length is the most direct way of reducing ambiguity about deployment times. Because stabilization will not always be practicable, improved communication should help personnel and their families stay in touch to cope with changes of plan.

Effect of Deployment on Nondeployed Personnel

Additional attention should be paid to the demands placed on nondeployed personnel by the increase in operational tempo.

Although our focus has been mainly on personnel who have deployed, we have also learned about nondeployed personnel. *Nondeployed personnel* in our terminology are personnel who are not currently deployed, who may be recovering from or preparing for a deployment, or who are not likely to deploy. Nondeployed personnel who were in our focus groups told us that many nondeployed personnel are affected by the increased operational tempo that accompanies the heightened pace of deployments. Nondeployed personnel often work long hours, with no leave, and are asked to perform additional duties to make up for the manpower lost when deployed personnel leave. In addition, those who deploy are often the most highly experienced personnel, leaving a young, less-proficient staff behind. The result is that some nondeployed personnel work as hard as those on deployments and spend large amounts of time away from their families, without many of the benefits of deployment, discussed above. Finally, nondeployed personnel face a challenge when their deployed colleagues return. Because they were not on the deployment and did not have the opportunity to form close personal bonds, personnel who did not deploy sometimes report being left out or unsure of their place within the unit.

Some personnel in our focus groups reported that these negative nondeployment experiences contribute to negative reenlistment attitudes. The effect of long work hours on work stress and reenlistment intentions was confirmed in our data analysis. These findings suggest that the military may want to devote additional resources to the support of nondeployed personnel, perhaps through the use of a "long hours" pay and through events or decorations to recognize the importance of their additional effort.

Training and Preparation

Effectively structured and focused training can help prepare members for difficult deployments and reduce the uncertainty surrounding deployments. The military should continue to revise and update its training programs to respond to the challenges of nontraditional conflicts.

The importance of effectively structured and executed training is an additional finding that emerges from this study. This finding is entirely consistent with past research on the importance of training and the relationship between stress and performance. Personnel in our focus groups reported that deployments were less stressful and more satisfying when they felt well prepared to do their jobs, trained for the tasks they were asked to carry out, and able to control their environment, at least to some extent.

Data analysis supported the relevance of self-perceived preparation to our measures of work stress and reenlistment intentions. Personnel in our focus groups, too, generally felt that their training provided them with important skills that helped them complete their jobs, both at home and on deployment. However, given the radical change in the nature of combat operations in recent years, military training must be continuously updated to assure personnel that they have the skills needed for their deployment. At the time of our focus groups in early 2004, personnel with whom we spoke said that more training on skills used in urban combat and counterinsurgency operations, such as conducting a raid, taking a hostage, or finding and avoiding snipers, were needed. Even personnel in our groups from the Air Force and the Navy, who tend to be less exposed to the dangers of combat, wanted to have more emergency-related training, such as how to put on a gas mask or fire a weapon.

These findings suggest the need for a highly adaptive training mechanism, one that has a short development cycle and is able to quickly incorporate new tactics and the demands of peacekeeping, stabilization, and counterinsurgency operations. Training should closely simulate the actual combat environment, including the presence of stressors, surprises, and casualties. The military services have drawn the same conclusion, and they have been revising their training programs to better simulate the conditions in places such as Iraq and Afghanistan.

Training targeted specifically at commanders is also relevant. Junior personnel in our groups reported that the quality and leadership of their commanders made a huge difference to morale and the overall experience of deployments. Expanding leadership programs to deployment-specific situations and using the expertise of those who have already deployed to a given location can develop the capability of commanders to lead personnel in difficult situations.

Combat Stress and Mental Health

Personnel returning from deployments report facing a range of personal, work, and combat-related stressors while on deployment. For some, the effects of these stressors are more long-term and significant than for others. Although some mental health resources exist, additional personnel support and counseling programs might be useful in preventing and treating mental health problems among service members.

According to personnel in our focus groups, current deployments and military life in general are characterized by periods of intense stress—personal, work, and combat-related. Long-term exposure to these types of (particularly combat-related) stressors can contribute to long-term mental health consequences. Preliminary research (Hoge et al., 2004) suggests that combat-stress reactions are affecting personnel returning from deployment, particularly those returning from long or back-to-back deployments. This finding is supported by focus group discussions.

Personnel in focus groups reported experiencing a range of problems when they returned from Iraq, including difficulty sleeping, strong reactions to loud noises, anger, excessive drinking, flashbacks to casualty situations, and anxiety. Most reported that they relied on their peers for help and relief during high-stress periods or following particularly traumatic situations. Many said that seeking help from professional counselors often has a stigma attached to it, and they questioned the usefulness of chaplains and other mental health counselors.

Extended services for returning members—for example, individual counseling or group classes, could be helpful in giving members the skills to deal with problems they may face after deployment, to understand their complex or extreme emotions, and to interact more effectively with their families. Such programs could also be used to identify personnel with more-severe problems so that they can receive additional help. Although the military services have begun to implement programs such as these, further expansion of these programs may be needed to ensure that all members, even those who live far from bases, have access to mental health care. Furthermore, steps need to be taken to ensure the confidentiality of mental health programs, meetings, and counseling and to remove the stigma associated with seeking this type of care, because lack of confidentiality and stigmatization have been identified as barriers to the receipt of necessary counseling.

As a major step in this direction, the services now screen all personnel returning from duty in Iraq and Afghanistan for indications of PTSD. The fact that the screening is mandatory removes the elements of stigma and self-selection. Other mental health programs and interventions, particularly those that deploy combat stress teams to the theater, have also proven themselves effective and should be applied widely—perhaps more widely than in the past, although we have not assessed their use. By addressing stress reactions at their source, such interventions can act as a preventive measure to reduce the number of personnel who return from deployment with undiagnosed mental health problems.

Although not as urgent, it would also be useful to assess whether and how additional counseling and stress-management resources would be useful for nondeployed personnel who have unusually heavy workloads. In addition, since most personnel rely on peers with whom to discuss their problems, it might be useful to determine whether additional training could make peers more effective in this role.

The military should ensure that mental health programs receive the resources (in personnel, funding, medicines, etc.) that they need to effectively treat and support service members. Continued tracking of mental health problems and stress reactions among personnel who have deployed or who have coped with a demanding workload would also seem to be a vital activity in itself and a worthwhile area of study. This type of research could provide a better understanding of the effect of current operations on deployed personnel and help to target future mental health programs at the most severe sources of problems. As with good training and effective leadership, it could also help support retention and, perhaps most important, help personnel deal with disturbing deployment experiences.

Further Research

We have suggested ways in which the military can improve the quality of life of deployed and nondeployed service members, consider the design and effectiveness of military family-support programs, and advance the preparedness of the force. The steps we suggest involve programs (family support, communications, stress management and mental health care, adaptive training, less ambiguity in deployment dates) and compensation (supplemental deployment pay for long or frequent deployments, additional pay for unusually long hours of work for the nondeployed).

Further research and analysis using more-recent data should be conducted to study how deployments affect the actual reenlistment of personnel, because the effect is an evolving and still-relevant question. Further research should also look for cost-effective ways to reduce the burden on service members—for example, changing the structure of military units, personnel-rotation policies, and job-assignment mechanisms.

Finally, many of our findings and suggestions are likely to be relevant to the Reserve forces. The effect of deployments on Reservists—on their expectations of the frequency, duration, and type of deployments; on the stress of separation from their civilian lives; on their jobs, career, and schooling; on their willingness to continue in service; and on their net pay gain or loss—deserves separate study. The issues and insights from our study may be applicable.

Expected-Utility Model of Deployment with Quadratic Utility

To illustrate the expected-utility model of deployment, we use a quadratic utility function. This function has the properties assumed in the model: that the marginal utility of each of the arguments in the utility function—i.e., income, home time, and deployment time—is positive, and that marginal utility is diminishing—i.e., it increases at a decreasing rate as each of the arguments increases. The quadratic utility function has a linear form and is easy to manipulate.

The quadratic utility function and expected utility function are expressed as follows:

$$U(d) = m + wd + a_1(1-d) - a_2(1-d)^2 + b_1 d - b_2 d^2 \tag{A.1}$$

$$EU(d) = (1-p)U(0) + p\int_{\mu-\delta}^{\mu+\delta} \frac{1}{2\delta} U(d)\, \mathrm{d}d \tag{A.2}$$

The parameters a_1, a_2, b_1, and b_2 are defined to be positive.

The preferred mean deployment time depends on deployment pay and factors affecting the marginal utility of time at home station and the marginal utility of time deployed.[1] As deployment time increases, the individual service member balances the increase in utility from additional deployment against the decrease in utility from less time at home station.

Because the quadratic utility function is symmetric, it has the property that the preferred mean deployment time equals the value of deployment time that maximizes the utility function. That value is found by setting the derivative of the utility function with respect to d equal to zero and solving for d^*, which gives:

$$d^* = \frac{w + 2a_2 + (b_1 - a_1)}{2(a_2 + b_2)} \tag{A.3}$$

---

[1] The quadratic utility function is additive in base pay and deployment pay. An implication of this additivity is that μ^* does not depend on base pay. However, if base pay and deployment pay entered the utility function as, say, $(m + wd)^\alpha$ instead of $(m + wd)$, then μ^* would depend on base pay.

Deployment pay and base pay have different effects on the preferred mean deployment time. At zero deployment pay, the preferred mean deployment time is zero if $2a_2 + (b_1 - a_1) \leq 0$. Increasing deployment pay to a positive amount moves the preferred mean to a positive value if the increase is large enough so that $w + 2a_2 + (b_1 - a_1) > 0$. If the preferred mean was positive at $w = 0$, adding deployment pay would again increase the preferred mean length of deployment. Either way, higher deployment pay increases the preferred mean.

In contrast, increasing base pay m does not affect the preferred mean length of deployment. In this utility function, the preferred mean deployment time is independent of m, as the formula shows. However, an increase in m or w will increase expected utility. An increase in m moves the utility curve vertically upward in a plot of utility against m, whereas an increase in w moves the curve upward and to the right in a plot of utility against w.

Means and Regressions

This appendix contains sample means and linear probability regressions for two dependent variables, higher-than-usual work stress and intention to stay in military service. Tables B.1 and B.2 contain the sample means, by branch of service, for enlisted personnel and for officers, respectively. Tables B.3 and B.4 present the results of linear probability regressions for higher-than-usual work stress, and Tables B.5 and B.6 present the results of linear probability regression for intention to remain on active duty, for enlisted personnel and officers, respectively. The order of the explanatory variables in the regressions parallels the order of discussion in Chapter Four.

The means and regressions are based on data from the March 2003 and July 2003 Status of Forces Surveys for active-duty personnel (Defense Manpower Data Center [DMDC], 2003a, b). The surveys were conducted by the DMDC via the Internet, and each survey had a response rate of 35 percent, resulting in sample sizes of 10,828 and 10,284, respectively. DMDC provided weights for the survey observations to make them representative of the active-duty population.[1]

The survey was based on stratified random sampling along dimensions including branch of service, officer/enlisted, pay grade category (E-1–E-4, E-5–E-9, W-1–W-5, O-1–O-3, O-4–O-6), location, race/ethnicity, education, family status, gender, and pay-grade category.[2] Within each branch of service, the sample count was at least 400 in each of these dimensions and was often over 1,000.

Survey documentation does not specify the size of the target population in the proportional random sampling frame. For this reason, we do not know the response rate within the sample frame groups, even though we know the respondent counts along the dimensions just mentioned. As a result, we do not know whether certain groups had unexpectedly low

---

[1] According to DMDC (2003a, p. 5),

> Data were weighted to reflect the population of interest. These weights reflect (1) the probability of selection, (2) a non-response adjustment factor to minimize bias arising from differential response rates among demographic subgroups, and (3) a post-stratification factor to force the response-adjusted weights to sum to the counts of the target population as of the month the sample was drawn and to provide additional non-response adjustments.

[2] According to DMDC (2003a, p. 5),

> In stratified random sampling, all members of a population are categorized into homogeneous groups. For example, members might be grouped by gender and Service (all male Army personnel in one group, all female Navy personnel in another, etc.). Members are chosen at random within each group. Small groups are oversampled in comparison to their proportion of the population so there will be enough respondents from small groups to analyze. Weights are generated so that estimates from the survey represent the population.

The weighting methodology is not further described in the documentation. We presumed, but did not find direct verification, that the dimensions listed in the text were used in weighting the data.

response rates or whether there was cause for concern about response bias. The Status of Forces Surveys, with a response rate of 35 percent, might or might not have response bias, just as a 70-percent-response-rate survey might or might not have response bias.

Response bias can occur if the respondents are not representative of the population in observed or unobserved ways. If not representative in an observed way, the data can be weighted, as was done. If perhaps not representative in unobserved ways, often little can be done to detect or correct this possible unrepresentativeness. Detection requires information from another source that includes the unobserved variables, in which case they can be included in the data analysis to see whether, for instance, regression estimates are affected by their inclusion/exclusion. We did not have an alternative data source to the Status of Forces surveys, and we cannot tell whether there is response bias from unobserved variables.

In analyzing the data, we computed both weighted and unweighted means. The variables we used were all indicator variables taking a value of either "0" or "1"; therefore, all variables' means fell between 0 and 1. The average difference between weighted and unweighted means was small, ranging from 0.004 to 0.026 across the eight groups used in our analysis (four services × enlisted and officer). Furthermore, the average difference was even smaller for variables not related to weighting. An example of such a variable is the indicator for whether the respondent worked longer than the usual duty-day 61–120 times in the past year. The difference in its mean using weighted versus unweighted data ranged from 0.001 to 0.017 across the eight groups.

For variables related to weighting, such as senior rank, marital status, and race/ethnicity, the average difference was considerably larger. For instance, the difference between the weighted and unweighted means for "female" was –0.109 for Army enlisted personnel, reflecting the fact that the survey sample frame oversampled women and, therefore, the fraction of women was 10.9 percent higher in the raw data than in the weighted data.

As mentioned in the main text, the omitted (or reference) group in the regressions was: worked longer than the usual duty-day 0–20 times; not away from permanent home station in the past 12 months; not in OEF/OIF combat operations; time away was neither more nor less than expected; you feel neither well nor poorly prepared; your unit is neither well nor poorly prepared; junior rank (E-1–E-4; O-1–O-3); not married; male; and self-reported race/ethnicity is white only.

The predicted probabilities in the Chapter Four tables use the omitted group as the reference group. Predictions can be easily made in a linear probability model by adding up the appropriate coefficients. For instance, in predicting the effect of the number of times worked longer than the usual duty-day, the intercept of the regression gives the probability for the base group, which includes worked longer 0–20 times for a member who was not away. The probability for a member who worked longer, say, more than 120 times, is found by adding the coefficient for that indicator to the intercept. The probability for a member who worked longer more than 120 times and was away, is found by the sum of the intercept, the coefficient on worked longer more than 120 times, the coefficient on the "away" indicator, and the coefficient on the "away*worked longer more than 120 times" indicator.

In contrast, models such as probit or logit regressions have a nonlinear relationship between the explanatory variables and the (implicit) dependent variable, which makes prediction less transparent.

Table B.1
Means: Enlisted Personnel

Variable	Army	Navy	Marine Corps	Air Force
<u>Dependent variables</u>				
Higher-than-usual personal stress	.47	.42	.42	.38
Higher-than-usual work stress	.56	.51	.50	.51
Likely to stay on active duty	.54	.60	.49	.64
Likely to stay on active duty for 20 or more years (03/03)[a]	.56	.62	.50	.65
Being away, or lack thereof, increased your desire to stay	.08	.09	.12	.10
Spouse thinks you should stay on active duty	.47	.49	.46	.52
Family thinks you should stay on active duty (03/07)[b]	.38	.47	.41	.50
Worked longer than usual duty-day in past 12 months				
0–20 times	.28	.42	.30	.38
21–60 times	.24	.23	.23	.24
61–120 times	.19	.14	.19	.15
>120 times	.29	.22	.28	.23
Away in past 12 months	.52	.39	.43	.37
Away*worked longer interactions				
Away*worked long 0–20 times	.08	.09	.07	.09
Away*worked long 21–60 times	.12	.09	.09	.09
Away*worked long 61–120 times	.11	.07	.10	.07
Away*worked long >120 times	.21	.14	.17	.11
In combat operations in OEF/OIF	.24	.16	.23	.12
Combat missing	.24	.19	.17	.18
Time away relative to expected time away				
Much less than expected	.10	.09	.15	.15
Less than expected	.13	.11	.16	.16
Neither more nor less than expected	.51	.55	.47	.53
More than expected	.15	.15	.12	.11
Much more than expected	.10	.11	.09	.06
Individual preparedness				
Very poorly prepared	.02	.01	.02	.01
Poorly prepared	.06	.03	.04	.04
Neither well nor poorly prepared	.13	.11	.11	.12
Well prepared	.43	.45	.43	.47
Very well prepared	.36	.39	.40	.36
Unit preparedness				
Very poorly prepared	.06	.01	.02	.01
Poorly prepared	.14	.06	.06	.05
Neither well nor poorly prepared	.24	.16	.17	.14
Well prepared	.41	.45	.45	.50
Very well prepared	.16	.32	.29	.30
Demographics				
Senior rank (E-5–E-9;O-4–O-6)	.50	.57	.38	.60
Married	.60	.53	.48	.59
Senior rank*married	.38	.40	.28	.46
Female	.14	.14	.06	.20
Minority or white/minority	.48	.43	.38	.35

SOURCE: Authors' tabulations.
[a]This variable was available only in the March 2003 survey (DMDC, 2003a).
[b]This variable was available only in the July 2003 survey (DMDC, 2003b).

Table B.2
Means: Officers

Variable	Army	Navy	Marine Corps	Air Force
Dependent variables				
Higher than usual personal stress	.41	.37	.36	.39
Higher than usual work stress	.50	.47	.40	.53
Likely to stay on active duty	.69	.72	.72	.71
Likely to stay on active duty for 20 or more years (03/03)[a]	.71	.72	.72	.70
Being away, or lack thereof, increased your desire to stay	.07	.09	.11	.09
Spouse thinks you should stay on active duty	.53	.57	.57	.57
Family thinks you should stay on active duty (03/07)[b]	.44	.50	.50	.52
Worked longer than usual duty-day in past 12 months				
0–20 times	.15	.26	.18	.20
21–60 times	.19	.21	.18	.20
61–120 times	.20	.18	.20	.18
>120 times	.46	.35	.43	.41
Away in past 12 months	.57	.49	.57	.53
Away*worked longer interactions				
Away*worked long 0–20 times	.04	.07	.04	.07
Away*worked long 21–60 times	.08	.09	.09	.11
Away*worked long 61–120 times	.12	.10	.12	.10
Away*worked long >120 times	.33	.23	.33	.25
In combat operations in OEF/OIF	.24	.22	.32	.22
Combat missing	.27	.24	.25	.24
Time away relative to expected time away				
Much less than expected	.06	.06	.08	.06
Less than expected	.16	.14	.18	.18
Neither more nor less than expected	.51	.60	.54	.54
More than expected	.16	.14	.14	.14
Much more than expected	.11	.06	.06	.08
Individual preparedness				
Very poorly prepared	.00	.00	.00	.02
Poorly prepared	.04	.03	.03	.06
Neither well nor poorly prepared	.11	.11	.10	.16
Well prepared	.49	.49	.44	.47
Very well prepared	.35	.36	.43	.30
Unit preparedness				
Very poorly prepared	.01	.01	.01	.01
Poorly prepared	.07	.05	.04	.05
Neither well nor poorly prepared	.23	.18	.18	.17
Well prepared	.48	.48	.46	.52
Very well prepared	.20	.29	.31	.25
Demographics				
Senior rank (E-5–E-9;O-4–O-6)	.45	.43	.39	.44
Married	.74	.71	.70	.74
Senior rank*married	.39	.37	.34	.38
Female	.14	.15	.05	.18
Minority or white/minority	.24	.18	.17	.18

SOURCE: Authors' tabulations.
[a] This variable was available only in the March 2003 survey (DMDC, 2003a).
[b] This variable was available only in the July 2003 survey (DMDC, 2003b).

Table B.3
Linear Probability Regression of Higher-Than-Usual Work Stress:
Enlisted Personnel (standard errors in parentheses; statistical significance on the right)

Variable	Army		Navy		Marine Corps		Air Force	
Intercept	.4448	***	.4856	***	.4273	***	.4123	***
	(.0350)		(.0407)		(.0447)		(.0382)	
Times worked longer than usual duty-day								
21–60	.1823	***	.2075	***	.1101	***	.1360	***
	(.0278)		(.0294)		(.0351)		(.0270)	
61–120	.2874	***	.2716	***	.2082	***	.2570	***
	(.0342)		(.0398)		(.0425)		(.0352)	
>120	.3046	***	.3141	***	.2865	***	.2951	***
	(.0310)		(.0379)		(.0377)		(.0304)	
Away from home base in past 12 months	−.0239		.0845	**	−.0554		−.0563	
	(.0366)		(.0402)		(.0496)		(.0361)	
Away*worked longer than usual duty-day								
21–60	−.0457		−.1369	***	−.0092		−.0229	
	(.0455)		(.0522)		(.0635)		(.0475)	
61–120	−.0472		−.1287	**	−.0130		−.0600	
	(.0500)		(.0613)		(.0678)		(.0551)	
>120	.0367		−.0829		−.0427		−.0106	
	(.0455)		(.0547)		(.0605)		(.0481)	
Served in combat operations in OEF/OIF	.0508		−.0157		−.0118		−.0916	*
	(.0345)		(.0455)		(.0439)		(.0484)	
Combat indicator missing	−.0084		−.0452		.0768	**	.0799	***
	(.0256)		(.0317)		(.0356)		(.0290)	
Time away less/greater than expected								
Much less than expected	−.0116		.0411		−.0499		−.0109	
	(.0278)		(.0340)		(.0320)		(.0258)	
Less than expected	−.0149		.0021		.0194		−.0336	
	(.0240)		(.0300)		(.0293)		(.0241)	
More than expected	.0728	***	.1095	***	.0392		.1316	***
	(.0239)		(.0292)		(.0360)		(.0303)	
Much more than expected	.1079	***	.1701	***	.0570		.0993	***
	(.0294)		(.0343)		(.0419)		(.0378)	

Table B.3—Continued

Variable	Army		Navy		Marine Corps		Air Force	
Individual preparedness								
Very poorly prepared	−.0133		−.0441		.0778		.1582	*
	(.0642)		(.0918)		(.0944)		(.0908)	
Poorly prepared	−.0181		.0108		.0898		.0143	
	(.0416)		(.0607)		(.0602)		(.0492)	
Well prepared	−.0452	*	−.0842	**	.0209		−.0264	
	(.0259)		(.0337)		(.0358)		(.0278)	
Very well prepared	−.1070	***	−.1101	***	.0659	*	−.0101	
	(.0280)		(.0362)		(.0391)		(.0308)	
Unit preparedness								
Very poorly prepared	.0750	*	.2019	**	.1856	**	.0331	
	(.0410)		(.0943)		(.0800)		(.0902)	
Poorly prepared	.1043	***	.1163	**	.0638		.1059	**
	(.0281)		(.0466)		(.0477)		(.0447)	
Well prepared	−.0214		−.0491	*	−.0493	*	—.0358	
	(.0208)		(.0284)		(.0297)		(.0269)	
Very well prepared	−.0406		−.0992	***	−.0877	**	−.0662	**
	(.0274)		(.0316)		(.0343)		(.0303)	
Senior rank	−.1017	***	−.0894	***	−.1136	***	.0522	*
	(.0278)		(.0297)		(.0352)		(.0280)	
Married	.0270		.0104		.0491		.0359	
	(.0261)		(.0322)		(.0317)		(.0281)	
Senior rank and married	−.0082		.0187		−.0533		−.0863	
	(.0350)		(.0410)		(.0462)		(.0372)	
Female	.0866	***	.0337		.0337		.0046	
	(.0191)		(.0248)		(.0256)		(.0195)	
Minority	−.0353	**	−.0015		−.0644	***	−.0285	*
	(.0191)		(.0248)		(.0256)		(.0195)	
R-squared	.1080		.1144		.0859		.0839	
Number of observations	11,363		7,320		5,180		9,167	

SOURCE: Authors' computations.
Statistical significance levels: *** = 0.01; ** = 0.05; * = 0.10.

Table B.4
Linear Probability Regression of Higher-Than-Usual Work Stress: Officers (standard errors in parentheses; statistical significance on the right)

Variable	Army		Navy		Marine Corps		Air Force	
Intercept	.2698	***	.3866	***	.2480	***	.3143	***
	(.0535)		(.0472)		(.0521)		(.0485)	
Times worked longer than usual duty-day								
21–60	.1230	***	.2237	***	.0353		.1452	***
	(.0453)		(.0408)		(.0470)		(.0453)	
61–120	.2672	***	.3149	***	.1856	***	.2575	***
	(.0513)		(.0466)		(.0503)		(.0465)	
>120	.3690	***	.3363	***	.3430	***	.3693	***
	(.0424)		(.0404)		(.0455)		(.0395)	
Away from home base in past 12 months	–.0400		.0108		.0285		–.1279	**
	(.0646)		(.0542)		(.0683)		(.0531)	
Away*worked longer than usual duty-day								
21–60	–.0652		–.1311	*	.0675		.0465	
	(.0793)		(.0696)		(.0833)		(.0685)	
61–120	–.0789		–.0776		–.0882		.0595	
	(.0802)		(.0715)		(.0835)		(.0710)	
>120	–.0649		–.0249		–.1018		.0601	
	(.0703)		(.0631)		(.0764)		(.0605)	
Served in combat operations in OEF/OIF	.0925	*	–.0326		–.1009	**	–.0295	
	(.0487)		(.0503)		(.0410)		(.0513)	
Combat indicator missing	.0435		.0298		.0449		.0386	
	(.0337)		(.0356)		(.0349)		(.0354)	
Time away less/greater than expected								
Much less than expected	–.0991	**	–.0214		–.0936	**	–.0611	
	(.0480)		(.0470)		(.0457)		(.0446)	
Less than expected	–.0371		–.0619	*	–.0872	***	–.0672	**
	(.0317)		(.0325)		(.0308)		(.0291)	
More than expected	.0710	**	–.0010		.0786	**	.1075	***
	(.0330)		(.0348)		(.0348)		(.0343)	
Much more than expected	.1410	***	.1397	***	.0986	**	.2037	***
	(.0403)		(.0502)		(.0487)		(.0461)	

Table B.4—Continued

Variable	Army		Navy		Marine Corps		Air Force	
Individual preparedness								
Very poorly prepared	.1201		−.1186		.0586		.0723	
	(.1483)		(.1795)		(.1853)		(.0921)	
Poorly prepared	.0593		−.0191		.0316		.0602	
	(.0639)		(.0768)		(.0742)		(.0511)	
Well prepared	−.0681	*	−.0689	*	−.0684		.0276	
	(.0384)		(.0405)		(.0427)		(.0337)	
Very well prepared	−.0565		−.0892	**	−.0952	**	.0360	
	(.0435)		(.0445)		(.0456)		(.0395)	
Unit preparedness								
Very poorly prepared	.1989	*	.2522	**	.1634		−.0193	
	(.1037)		(.1216)		(.1284)		(.1300)	
Poorly prepared	.1186	**	.0424		.1188	*	.0757	
	(.0485)		(.0600)		(.0650)		(.0563)	
Well prepared	.0590	**	.0071		.0561	*	−.0023	
	(.0284)		(.0340)		(.0329)		(.0313)	
Very well prepared	.0171		−.0754	*	.0233		−.0497	
	(.0376)		(.0394)		(.0378)		(.0384)	
Senior rank	−.0102		−.0784		.1095	*	−.0265	
	(.0497)		(.0494)		(.0567)		(.0477)	
Married	−.0025		−.0323		.0297		.0154	
	(.0334)		(.0327)		(.0328)		(.0319)	
Senior rank and married	.0285		.0957		−.0663		−.0013	
	(.0556)		(.0552)		(.0618)		(.0535)	
Female	.0619	**	−.0022		.0188		.0488	*
	(.0271)		(.0300)		(.0501)		(.0265)	
Minority	−.0541	**	−.0179		−.0059		−.0583	**
	(.0271)		(.0300)		(.0501)		(.0265)	
R-squared	.1156		.0981		.0842		.1215	
Number of observations	8,618		5,585		4,333		7,470	

SOURCE: Authors' computations.
Statistical significance levels: *** = 0.01; ** = 0.05; * = 0.10.

Table B.5
Linear Probability Regression of Intention to Stay on Active Duty: Enlisted Personnel
(standard errors in parentheses; statistical significance on the right)

Variable	Army		Navy		Marines		Air Force	
Intercept	.3625	***	.3278	***	.2938	***	.4056	***
	(.0341)		(.0386)		(.0414)		(.0361)	
Times worked longer than usual duty-day								
21–60	–.0259		–.0195		–.0686	**	–.0441	*
	(.0271)		(.0279)		(.0325)		(.0256)	
61–120	–.0637	*	–.1186	***	–.1407	***	–.0611	*
	(.0333)		(.0377)		(.0394)		(.0334)	
>120	–.0900	***	–.0828	**	–.0121		–.0973	***
	(.0302)		(.0359)		(.0349)		(.0288)	
Away from home base in past 12 months	.0098		–.0265		–.0220		–.0141	
	(.0356)		(.0383)		(.0460)		(.0343)	
Away*worked longer than usual duty-day								
21–60	–.0763	*	–.0529		–.0557		–.0063	
	(.0444)		(.0495)		(.0587)		(.0450)	
61–120	–.0291		.0768		.0377		.0101	
	(.0487)		(.0581)		(.0628)		(.0522)	
>120	–.0445		.0811		–.1429	**	.0210	
	(.0443)		(.0519)		(.0561)		(.0456)	
Served in combat operations in OEF/OIF	–.0646	*	.0116		.0095		–.0076	
	(.0337)		(.0432)		(.0407)		(.0459)	
Combat indicator missing	.0776	***	.0203		.0626	*	.0719	***
	(.0250)		(.0301)		(.0330)		(.0275)	
Time away less/greater than expected								
Much less than expected	–.0187		–.0049		–.0090		.0378	
	(.0271)		(.0323)		(.0297)		(.0244)	
Less than expected	.0303		.0067		–.0212		–.0018	
	(.0234)		(.0285)		(.0271)		(.0228)	
More than expected	–.0043		–.0534	*	–.0200		–.0263	
	(.0233)		(.0277)		(.0333)		(.0287)	
Much more than expected	–.0565	**	–.1532	***	–.0238		–.1623	***
	(.0286)		(.0325)		(.0387)		(.0359)	

Table B.5—Continued

Variable	Army		Navy		Marine Corps		Air Force	
Individual preparedness								
Very poorly prepared	−.0808		−.1360		−.0774		−.1542	*
	(.0625)		(.0870		(.0874)		(.0841)	
Poorly prepared	−.0049		.0174		−.0005		.0221	
	(.0406)		(.0578		(.0557)		(.0466)	
Well prepared	.0577	**	.1264	***	.0724	**	.0718	***
	(.0252)		(.0320		(.0331)		(.0264)	
Very well prepared	.0911	***	.1752	***	.1013	***	.1075	***
	(.0273)		(.0343		(.0362)		(.0292)	
Unit preparedness								
Very poorly prepared	−.0893	**	−.0248		−.1290	*	−.1636	*
	(.0401)		(.0894		(.0740)		(.0845)	
Poorly prepared	−.0228		−.1378	***	−.0287		−.0886	**
	(.0274)		(.0443		(.0442)		(.0423)	
Well prepared	.0595	***	.0022		.0116		.0637	**
	(.0203)		(.0269		(.0275)		(.0255)	
Very well prepared	.0794	***	.0564	*	.0703	**	.0859	***
	(.0267)		(.0299		(.0318)		(.0287)	
Senior rank	.2731	***	.2019	***	.2829	***	.2160	***
	(.0271)		(.0282		(.0326)		(.0265)	
Married	.0264		.1183	***	.0491	*	.0460	*
	(.0254)		(.0305		(.0294)		(.0266)	
Senior rank and married	−.0127		−.0022		.0958		.0155	
	(.0341)		(.0389		(.0428)		(.0352)	
Female	−.0496	***	.0163		−.0464	*	.0055	
	(.0186)		(.0235		(.0238)		(.0185)	
Minority	.0650	***	.0579	***	.0868	***	−.0183	
	(.0186)		(.0235		(.0238)		(.0185)	
R-squared	.1210		.1318		.2063		.0945	
Number of observations	3,623		2,600		2,158		3,241	

SOURCE: Authors' computations.
Statistical significance levels: *** = 0.01; ** = 0.05; * = 0.10.

**Table B.6
Linear Probability Regression of Intention to Stay on Active Duty: Officers
(standard errors in parentheses; statistical significance on the right)**

Variable	Army		Navy		Marines		Air Force	
Intercept	.6219	***	.5342	***	.5531	***	.5837	***
	(.0494)		(.0424)		(.0478)		(.0454)	
Times worked longer than usual duty-day								
21–60	−.0810	*	.0015		−.0714	*	−.0191	
	(.0418)		(.0367)		(.0430)		(.0424)	
61–120	−.1439	***	.0034		−.0522		−.0973	**
	(.0473)		(.0418)		(.0460)		(.0436)	
>120	−.1216	***	−.0003		−.0842	**	−.0643	*
	(.0391)		(.0362)		(.0416)		(.0370)	
Away from home base in past 12 months	−.0479		.0697		−.0004		.0723	
	(.0595)		(.0487)		(.0623)		(.0497)	
Away*worked longer than usual duty-day								
21–60	.0573		−.0127		−.0139		−.0051	
	(.0731)		(.0625)		(.0761)		(.0642)	
61–120	.1153		−.0682		−.0638		.0420	
	(.0738)		(.0642)		(.0763)		(.0665)	
>120	.0520		−.0440		−.0157		−.0432	
	(.0647)		(.0566)		(.0698)		(.0567)	
Served in combat operations in OEF/OIF	−.1170	***	−.0244		−.0382		.0208	
	(.0447)		(.0452)		(.0375)		(.0481)	
Combat indicator missing	.0628	**	.0128		.0551	*	−.0112	
	(.0310)		(.0320)		(.0318)		(.0332)	
Time away less/greater than expected								
Much less than expected	−.0206		−.0366		−.0108		.0029	
	(.0442)		(.0422)		(.0415)		(.0418)	
Less than expected	−.0530	*	.0408		−.0158		.0031	
	(.0292)		(.0292)		(.0282)		(.0272)	
More than expected	−.0414		.0107		−.0211		−.0935	***
	(.0304)		(.0312)		(.0318)		(.0321)	
Much more than expected	−.1377	***	−.1592	***	−.0959	**	−.1479	***
	(.0370)		(.0451)		(.0446)		(.0432)	

Table B.6—Continued

Variable	Army		Navy		Marines		Air Force	
Individual preparedness								
Very poorly prepared	−.1974		−.0018		−.2168		−.0407	
	(.1365)		(.1613)		(.1692)		(.0862)	
Poorly prepared	−.1087	*	−.0341		−.1129	*	−.0324	
	(.0588)		(.0690)		(.0678)		(.0478)	
Well prepared	.0755	**	.0466		.1046	***	.0800	**
	(.0355)		(.0363)		(.0390)		(.0315)	
Very well prepared	.0827	**	.0150		.1112	***	.0725	*
	(.0401)		(.0399)		(.0416)		(.0370)	
Unit preparedness								
Very poorly prepared	−.0929		−.2711	**	−.1462		−.2093	*
	(.0954)		(.1092)		(.1173)		(.1217)	
Poorly prepared	−.0914	**	−.1627	***	−.1060	*	−.0488	
	(.0446)		(.0539)		(.0593)		(.0527)	
Well prepared	.0267		.0854	***	.0906	***	−.0041	
	(.0261)		(.0305)		(.0301)		(.0293)	
Very well prepared	.0940	***	.1021	***	.1171	***	.0757	**
	(.0346)		(.0353)		(.0346)		(.0360)	
Senior rank	.2156	***	.1778	***	.0993	*	.1300	***
	(.0457)		(.0443)		(.0518)		(.0446)	
Married	.1184	***	.0860	***	.0872	***	.0639	**
	(.0308)		(.0294)		(.0300)		(.0298)	
Senior rank and married	−.1345		−.1163		−.0559		−.0316	
	(.0512)		(.0496)		(.0564)		(.0501)	
Female	−.0461	*	−.0700	***	−.0931	**	−.0344	
	(.0250)		(.0269)		(.0457)		(.0248)	
Minority	.0005		.0515	**	.0595	**	.0436	*
	(.0250)		(.0269)		(.0457)		(.0248)	
R-squared	.0959		.0675		.0714		.0591	
Number of observations	1,913		1,944		1,843		1,973	

SOURCE: Authors' computations.
Statistical significance levels: *** = 0.01; ** = 0.05; * = 0.10.

Distribution of Number of Times Service Members Reported Working Longer Than the Usual Duty-Day

The March 2003 and July 2003 Status of Forces Survey (Defense Manpower Data Center, 2003a, b) for active-duty personnel asked service members to indicate the number of times in the past 12 months that they had worked longer than the usual duty-day. The survey instrument did not define the length of the usual duty-day, and the responses to this question should be viewed as reflecting the judgment of the respondent on what constitutes a *normal duty-day*. Similarly, the survey instrument did not provide guidance on what a normal duty-day might be during a deployment versus a normal duty-day at a permanent duty station (when not deployed). Table C.1 tabulates the responses for enlisted and officer personnel by branch of service and by whether the service member reported being away from his or her permanent duty station within the 12 months preceding the survey.

Table C.1
Number of Times Worked Longer Than the Usual Duty-Day in the Past 12 Months

Times worked longer than the usual duty-day	Army		Navy		Marine Corps		Air Force	
	Not away	Away	Not away	Away	Not away	Away	Not away	Away
Enlisted								
Zero	8%	3%	18%	7%	12%	4%	10%	4%
1–10	18%	6%	22%	8%	16%	7%	20%	11%
11–20	13%	7%	13%	9%	13%	6%	16%	8%
21–60	26%	23%	23%	24%	25%	23%	25%	26%
61–120	14%	21%	10%	19%	15%	22%	13%	21%
>120	20%	40%	13%	33%	20%	38%	17%	30%
	100%	100%	100%	100%	100%	100%	100%	100%
Officer								
Zero	7%	2%	13%	3%	11%	1%	7%	3%
1–10	10%	3%	15%	4%	10%	2%	9%	5%
11–20	9%	3%	11%	7%	10%	4%	10%	6%
21–60	24%	15%	24%	19%	22%	17%	20%	21%
61120	18%	21%	14%	21%	18%	20%	18%	19%
>120	32%	57%	23%	46%	29%	56%	35%	46%
	100%	100%	100%	100%	100%	100%	100%	100%

SOURCE: Authors' tabulations.

Bibliography

Adams, J., *The Stability of Trait Anxiety and State Anxiety Responses to Coping Skills Training,* Doctoral Dissertation, Kent State University, Ann Arbor, Mich.: Dissertation Abstracts International, 42/42B, 1579, 1981.

Adler, A., and C. Castro, *US Soldiers and Peacekeeping Deployments,* Frederick, Md.: U.S. Army Medical Research and Material Command, 2001.

Adler, A., et al., *US Soldier Study III: Kosovo Post Deployment,* Heidelberg, Germany: U.S. Army Medical Research Unit–Europe, USAMRU-E Technical Brief 00-04, 2000.

Adler, A., M. Vaitkus, and J. Martin, "Combat Exposure and Posttraumatic Stress Symptomatology Among US Soldiers Deployed to the Gulf War," *Military Psychology,* Vol. 8, 1996, pp. 1–14.

Adlerks, Cathie, *PERSTEMPO: Its Effects on Soldiers' Attitudes,* Alexandria, Va.: U.S. Army Research Institute for the Behavioral and Social Sciences, Study Report 98-02, 1992.

Altmaier, E., and D. Happ, "Coping Skills Training's Immunization Effects Against Learned Helplessness," *Journal of Social and Clinical Psychology,* Vol. 3, 1985, pp. 181–189.

Applewhite, Larry W., and David R. Segal, "Telephone Use by Peacekeeping Troops in the Sinai," *Armed Forces & Society,* Vol. 17, No. 1, Fall 1990, pp. 117–126.

"Army to Recall Former Military Members," Associated Press, June 29, 2004.

Arsenault, A., and S. Dolan, "The Role of Personality, Occupation, and Organization in Understanding the Relationship Between Job Stress, Performance, Absenteeism," *Journal of Occupational Psychology,* Vol. 56, 1983, pp. 27–240.

Avant, Deborah, and James Lebovic, "U.S. Military Attitudes Toward Post–Cold War Missions," *Armed Forces & Society,* Vol. 27, No. 1, Fall 2000, pp. 37–56.

Balzar, John, "Doubts and Duty Tug at Marines," *Los Angeles Times,* July 6, 2004, p. A1.

Barron, R., and D. Kenny, "The Moderator-Mediator Variable Distinction in Social Psychological Research: Conceptual, Strategic, and Statistical Considerations," *Journal of Personality and Social Psychology,* Vol. 51, 1986, pp. 1173–1182.

Barry, Ellen, "Taking Their Couches to Iraq," *Los Angeles Times,* August 9, 2004.

Bell, Bruce D., Walter R. Schumm, Benjamin Knott, and Morten G. Ender, "The Desert Fax: A Research Note on Calling Home from Somalia," *Armed Forces & Society,* Vol. 25, No. 3, Spring 1999, pp. 509–521.

Board on Behavioral, Cognitive, and Sensory Sciences and Education, *Attitudes, Aptitudes, and Aspirations of American Youth: Implications for Military Recruitment,* Washington, D.C.: National Research Council, Division on Behavioral and Social Sciences and Education, 2003.

Boesel, David, and Kyle Johnson, *Why Service Members Leave the Military: A Review of the Literature and Analysis,* Washington, D.C.: Defense Manpower Data Center, Personnel Survey Branch, DMDC/MTC/TR-84-3, April 1984.

Bourg, Chris, and Mady Wechsler Segal, "The Impact of Family Supportive Policies and Practices on Organizational Commitment to the Army," *Armed Forces & Society,* Vol. 25, No. 4, Summer 1999, pp. 633–652.

Bowers, Clint, Jeanne Weaver, and Ben Morgan, "Moderating the Performance Effects of Stress," in James Driskell and Eduardo Salas, eds., *Stress and Human Performance,* New Jersey: Lawrence Erlbaum Associates, 1996, pp. 163–192.

Brewer, M. B., "In-Group Bias in the Minimal Intergroup Situation: A Cognitive-Motivational Analysis," *Psychological Bulletin,* Vol. 86, 1979, pp. 307–324.

Briner, Bob B., and Shirley Reynolds, "The Costs, Benefits and Limitations of Organizational Level Stress Interventions," *Journal of Organizational Behavior,* Vol. 20, 1999, pp. 647–664.

Britt, T., and A. Adler, "Stress and Health During Medical Humanitarian Assistance Missions," *Military Medicine,* Vol. 164, No. 4, 1999, pp. 275–279.

Bruce, Reginald, and Regina Burch, *Officer Career Development: Modeling Married Aviator Retention,* San Diego, Calif.: Navy Personnel Research and Development Center, Technical Report 89-11, 1989.

Brush, Silla, "Military Enlistees Not Overly Concerned About War," *Dallas Morning News,* June 21, 2004.

Bulkeley, William, "Mental Ills Rise Among Soldiers Back from Iraq," *The Wall Street Journal,* July 1, 2004, p. B4.

Burrell, Lolita, Doris Durand, and Jennifer Fortado, "Military Community Integration and Its Effect on Well-Being and Retention," *Armed Forces & Society,* Vol. 30, No., 1, Fall 2003, pp. 7–24.

Campbell, Major Spencer, Captain Darren Ritzer, Sergeant John Valentine, and Colonel Robert Gifford, *Operation Joint Guard, Bosnia: An Assessment of Operational Stress and Adaptive Coping Mechanisms of Soldiers,* Washington, D.C.: Walter Reed Institute of Research, 1998.

Caplan, Robert, and Kenneth Jones, "Effects of Work Load, Role Ambiguity, and Type A Personality on Anxiety, Depression, and Heart Rate," *Journal of Applied Psychology,* Vol. 60, No. 6, 1975, pp. 713–719.

Chow, Winston, and J. Michael Polich, *Models of the First-Term Reenlistment Decision,* Santa Monica, Calif.: RAND Corporation, R-2468-MRAL, 1980.

Cline, V. B., et al., "A Survey of Opinions Regarding Operation Gyroscope in the First Division," Staff memorandum, Washington, D.C.: Human Resources Research Office, George Washington University, 1955. In Little (1971).

Cohen, David Michael, "Training for the Sound and the Fury," *San Antonio Express-News,* June 12, 2004.

Corbett, Sara, "The Permanent Scars of Iraq," *New York Times Magazine,* February 15, 2004.

Cropanzano, Russell, Deborah Rapp, and Zinta Bryne, "The Relationship of Emotional Exhaustion to Work Attitudes, Job Performance, and Organizational Citizenship Behaviors," *Journal of Applied Psychology,* Vol. 88, No. 1, February 2003, pp. 160–169.

Davey, Monica, "For Soldiers Back from Iraq, Basic Training in Resuming Life," *The New York Times,* May 31, 2004.

Defense Manpower Data Center, March 2003 Status of Forces Survey of Active-Duty Members: Tabulations of Responses, Seaside, Calif.: DMDC Report No. 2003-004, July 2003a.

————, July 2003 Status of Forces Survey of Active-Duty Members: Tabulations of Responses, Seaside, Calif.: DMDC Report No. 2003-019, November 2003b.

Deffenbacher, J., and R. Hahnloser, "Cognitive and relaxation coping skills in Stress Inoculation," *Cognitive Therapy and Research*, Vol. 2, 1981, pp. 211–215.

Deikis, J., *Stress Inoculation Training: Effects of Anxiety, Self-Efficacy, and Performance in Divers*, Doctoral Dissertation, Temple University, Ann Arbor, Mich.: Dissertation Abstracts International, 44/1B, 303, 1982.

DMDC—see Defense Manpower Data Center.

Driskell, James, Rhonwyn Carson, and Patrick Moskal, *Stress and Human Performance: A Final Report*, Orlando, Fla., Naval Air Warfare Training Systems Center, August 15, 1988.

Driskell, J., R. Hogan, and E. Salas, "Personality and Group Performance," in C. Hendrick, ed., *Group Processes and Intergroup Relations*, Newbury Park, Calif.: Sage, 1987.

Driskell, James, and Joan Johnston, "Stress Exposure Training," in Janis Cannon-Bowers and Eduardo Salas, eds., *Making Decisions Under Stress*, Washington D.C.: American Psychological Association, 1998, pp. 191–217.

Duhigg, Charles, " 'Enemy Contact. Kill 'Em, Kill 'Em,'" *Los Angeles Times*, July 18, 2004.

Dwyer, Timothy, "Wounded Soldiers Are Adapting to Altered Lives," *Washington Post*, August 11, 2004, p. A1.

Easterbrook, J., "The Effect of Emotion on Cue Utilization and Organization of Behavior," *Psychological Review*, Vol. 66, 1959, pp. 183–201.

Edwards J., and R. Van Harrison, "Job Demands and Worker Health: Three Dimensional Reexamination of the Relationship Between Person-Environment Fit and Strain," *Journal of Applied Psychology*, Vol. 78, No. 4, August 1993, pp. 628–648.

Emert, Rick, "Mental Health Pros Say Biggest Challenge in Treating Stress Is Getting Soldiers to Ask for Help," *European Stars and Stripes*, July 25, 2004.

Ender, Morten G., "G.I. Phone Home: The Use of Telecommunications by the Soldiers of Operation Just Cause," *Armed Forces & Society*, Vol. 21, No. 3, Spring 1995, pp. 435–453.

————, "E-mail to Somalia: New Communication Media Between Home and War Fronts," in Joseph E. Behar, ed., *Mapping Cyberspace: Social Research on the Electronic Frontier*, Oakdale, N.Y.: Dowling College Press, 1997, pp. 27–52.

————, "The Postmodern Military: Soldiering, New Media, and the Post–Cold War," *Journal for the Study of Peace and Conflict*, 1997–1998 Annual Edition, pp. 50–58.

Enns, John, *Reenlistment Bonuses and First-Term Retention*, Santa Monica, Calif.: RAND Corporation, R-1935-ARPA, 1977.

Finger, R., and J. Galassi, "Effects of Modifying Cognitive Versus Emotionality Responses in the Treatment of Test Anxiety," *Journal of Consulting and Clinical Psychology*, Vol. 45, 1977, pp. 280–287.

Fisher, Franklin, "Air Force Program Aims to Nip Combat Stress in the Bud," *Pacific Stars and Stripes*, July 26, 2004.

Foa, E., R. Zinbarg, and B. Rothbaum, "Uncontrollability and Unpredictability in Post-Traumatic Stress Disorder: An Animal Model," *Psychological Bulletin*, Vol. 112, 1992, pp. 218–238.

Franke, Volker, "Warriors for Peace: The Next Generation of Military Leaders," *Armed Forces & Society*, Vol. 24, No. 1, 1997, pp. 33–57.

Fricker, Ron, *The Effects of PERSTEMPO on Officer Retention in the U.S. Military*, Santa Monica, Calif.: RAND Corporation, MR-1556-OSD, 2002.

Friedland, Nehemia, and Giora Keinan, "Training Effective Performance in Stressful Situations: Three Approaches and Implications for Combat Training," *Military Psychology*, Vol. 4, No. 3, 1992, pp. 157–174.

Friedman, L., "How Affiliation Affects Stress in Fear and Anxiety Situations," *Journal of Personality and Social Psychology*, Vol. 40, 1981, pp. 1102–1117.

Fussell, Paul, *The Great War and Modern Memory*, New York: Oxford University Press, 1975.

Gaertner, S. L., et al., "The Common Intergroup Identity Model: Recategorization and the Reduction of Intergroup Bias," in W. Stroebe and M. Hewstone, eds., *European Review of Sociology*, Vol. 4, 1993.

Gaillard, A., and F. Steyvers, "Sleep Loss and Sustained Performance," in A. Coblentz, ed., *Vigilance and Performance in Automatized Systems*, Dordrecht: Kluwer Academic Publishers, 1989.

Glass, David, and Jerome Singer, "Experimental Studies of Uncontrollable and Unpredictable Noise," *Representative Research in Social Psychology*, Vol. 4, No. 1, January 1972, pp. 165–183.

Goldberg, Matthew, *A Survey of Enlisted Retention: Models and Findings*, Alexandria, Va.: Center for Naval Analyses, 2001.

Goldberg, Matthew, and John Warner, *Determinants of Navy Reenlistment and Extension Rates*, Alexandria, Va.: Center for Naval Analyses, December 1982.

Golding, Heidi, and Henry Griffis, *Increased PERSTEMPO, Retention, and Navy Policy*, Washington, D.C.: Center for Naval Analyses, 2003.

———, *Offsetting the Negative Retention Effects of Long Deployments*, Alexandria, Va.: Center for Naval Analyses, CNA Memorandum 5125, 2001.

Golding, Heidi, et al., *Fleet Attrition: What Causes It and What to Do About It*, Alexandria, Va.: Center for Naval Analyses, 2001.

Green, B., et al., "Risk Factors for PTSD and Other Diagnoses in a General Sample of Vietnam Veterans," *American Journal of Psychiatry*, Vol. 147, 1990, pp. 729–733.

Griffis, Henry, Anita Hattiangadi, and David Gregory, *"Can Do" No More? An Assessment of Seabee Compensation*, Alexandria, Va.: Center for Naval Analyses, 2002.

Griffith, James, "The Army's New Unit Personnel Replacement and Its Relationship to Unit Cohesion and Social Support," *Military Psychology*, Vol. 1, No. 1, 1998, pp. 17–34.

"Gulf War Deployments," Washington, D.C.: U.S. Department of Defense, Deployment Health Clinical Center. Available online at http://www.pdhealth.mil/deployments/gulfwar/background.asp#events; accessed February 2, 2005.

Halverson, Ronald R., and Paul D. Bliese, "Determinants of Soldier Support for Operation Uphold Democracy," *Armed Forces & Society*, Vol. 23, No. 1, Fall 1996, pp.81–96.

Halverson, Captain Ronald, Captain Paul Bliese, Sergeant Robert Moore, and Captain Carl Castro, *Psychological Well-Being and Physical Health Symptoms Deployed for Operation Uphold Democracy: A Summary of Human Dimensions Research in Haiti*, Washington D.C.: Walter Reed Army Institute for Research, 1995.

Hatton, C., et al., "Stressors, Coping Strategies, and Stress Related Outcomes Among Direct Care Staff in Staffed Houses for People with Learning Disabilities," *Mental Handicap Research,* Vol. 8, 1995, pp. 252–271.

Helmus, Todd, and Russell Glenn, *Steeling the Mind: Combat Stress Reactions and Their Implications for Urban Warfare,* Santa Monica, Calif.: RAND Corporation, MG-191-A, 2005.

Henderson, W. Darryl, *Cohesion: The Human Element in Combat,* Washington, D.C.: National Defense University Press, 1985.

———, *The Hollow Army,* New York: Greenwood Press, 1990.

Herzog, Tobey C., *Vietnam War Stories,* New York: Routledge, 1992.

Hoge, Charles, Carl Castro, Stephen Messer, et al., "Combat Duty in Iraq and Afghanistan, Mental Health Problems, Barriers to Care," *New England Journal of Medicine,* Vol. 351, No. 1, July 1, 2004, pp. 13–22.

Hogg, M. A., *The Social Psychology of Group Cohesiveness: From Attraction to Social Identity,* New York: New York University Press, 1992.

Hosek, James, *Deployment, Retention, and Compensation,* Santa Monica, Calif.: RAND Corporation, CT-222, 2004.

Hosek, James, and Christine Peterson, *Reenlistment Bonuses and Retention Behavior: Executive Summary,* Santa Monica, Calif.: RAND Corporation, R-3199-MIL, 1985.

Hosek, James, and Mark Totten, *Does Perstempo Hurt Reenlistment? The Effect of Long or Hostile Perstempo on Reenlistment,* Santa Monica, Calif.: RAND Corporation, MR-990-OSD, 1998.

———, *Serving Away from Home: How Deployments Influence Reenlistment,* Santa Monica, Calif.: RAND Corporation, MR-1594-OSD, 2002.

Huffman, A., A. Adler, and C. Castro, *USAREUR/7A OPTEMPO and PERSTEMPO Study—In Progress Report,* Heidelberg, Germany: U.S. Army Medical Research Center, USAMRU-E Technical Brief 00-06, 2000.

Huffman, Ann H., Amy B. Adler, Carol A. Dolan, Jeffrey L. Thomas, and Carl A. Castro, *Impact of OPTEMPO on Retention of U.S. Personnel in Europe,* Heidelberg, Germany: U.S. Army Medical Research and Material Command, U.S. Army Medical Research Unit–Europe, Walter Reed Army Institute of Research, OPTEMPO Report Series #11, November 28, 2001a.

———, "Impact of OPTEMPO on Retention of US Personnel in Europe," Silver Spring, Md.: U.S. Army Medical Research Unit, Presented at the American Psychological Association Annual Meeting, San Francisco, Calif., November 2001b.

Huffstutter, P. J., "Far from Soldiers of Fortune," *Los Angeles Times,* May 12, 2004, p. 1.

Hytten, K., A. Jensen, and G. Skauli, "Stress Inoculation Training for Smoke Divers and Free Fall Lifeboat Passengers," *Aviation, Space, and Environmental Medicine,* Vol. 61, 1990, pp. 983–988.

Idzikowski, C., and A. Baddeley, "Fear and Dangerous Environments," in R. Hockey, ed., *Stress and Fatigue in Human Performance,* Chichester, United Kingdom: Wiley Press, 1983, pp. 123–144.

Jaffe, Greg, "As Ranks Dwindle in a Reserve Unit, Army's Woes Mount," *The Wall Street Journal,* August 4, 2004, p. A1.

Jamal, M., "Relationship of Job Stress to Job Performance: A Study of Managers and Blue-Collar Workers," *Human Relations,* Vol. 38, 1985, pp. 409–425.

Janis, Irving, *Groupthink: Psychological Studies of Policy Decisions and Fiascoes,* 2nd Ed., Boston, Mass.: Houghton Mifflin, 1983.

Janis, Irving, and Leon Mann, *Decision Making,* New York: Free Press, 1977.

Janowitz, Morris, *The Professional Soldier,* New York: Free Press, 1960.

Jex, Steve, and Paul Bliese, "Efficacy as a Moderator of the Impact of Work-Related Stressors: A Multilevel Study," *Journal of Applied Psychology,* Vol. 84, No. 3, 1999, pp. 349–361.

Johns, J. H., et al. (Defense Management Study Group on Military Cohesion), *Cohesion in the US Military,* Washington, D.C.: National Defense University Press, 1984.

Johnson, D. W., et al., "Effects of Cooperative, Competitive, and Individualistic Goal Structures on Achievement: A Meta-Analysis," *Psychological Bulletin,* Vol. 89, 1981, pp. 47–192.

Johnson, D. W., R. Johnson, and G. Maruyama, "Goal Interdependence and Interpersonal Attraction in Heterogeneous Classrooms: A Meta-Analysis," in N. Miller and M. Brewer, eds., *Groups in Contact: The Psychology of Desegregation,* New York: Academic Press, 1984, Chapter 9, pp. 187–212.

Johnson, L., D. Cline, J. Marcum, et al., "Effectiveness of a Stress Recovery Unit During the Persian Gulf War" *Hospital Community Psychiatry,* Vol. 43, 1992, pp. 829–831.

Johnson, Patti Major, *Social Environment and Stress Factors That Relate to Well-Being, Satisfaction, and Attitudes Toward Retention and Deployability in Married and Single Parent Female Soldiers,* Washington, D.C.: Walter Reed Army Medical Center, 1996.

Johnston, Joan, and Janis Cannon-Bowers, "Training for Stress Exposure," in James Driskell and Eduardo Salas, eds., *Stress and Human Performance,* Mahwah, N.J.: Lawrence Erlbaum Associates, 1996, pp. 223–256.

Johnston, Joan, Richard Poirier, and Kimberly Smith Jentsch, "Decision-making Under Stress: Creating a Research Methodology," in Janis Cannon-Bowers and Eduardo Salas, eds., *Making Decisions Under Stress,* Washington D.C.: American Psychological Association, 1998, pp. 9–59.

Jöreskog, K., and A. S. Goldberger, "Estimation of a Model with Multiple Indicators and Multiple Causes of a Single Latent Variable," *Journal of American Statistical Association,* Vol. 70, 1975, pp. 631–639.

Judd, C. M., and D. A. Kenny, "Process Analysis: Estimating Mediation in Treatment Evaluations," *Evaluation Review,* Vol. 5, No. 5, 1981, pp. 602–619.

Kahan, J. P., N. Webb, R. J. Shavelson, and R. M. Stolzenberg, *Individual Characteristics and Unit Performance: A Review of Research and Methods,* Santa Monica, Calif.: RAND Corporation, R-3194-MIL, 1985.

Kahana, B., Z. Harel, and F. Kahana, "Predictors of Psychological Well-Being Among Survivors of the Holocaust," in J. Wilson, ed., *Human Adaptation to Extreme Stress: From the Holocaust to Vietnam,* New York: Plenum, 1988, pp. 171–192.

Kavanagh, Jennifer, *Stress and Performance: A Review of the Literature and Its Applicability to the Military,* Santa Monica, Calif.: RAND Corporation, TR-192-RC, 2005.

Kellet, Anthony, *Combat Motivation: The Behavior of Soldiers in Battle,* Boston, Mass.: Kluwer, 1982.

Kelley, Eileen, "7,000 Fort Carson Troops Are Ordered to Return to Iraq," *Denver Post,* July 8, 2004.

Kelley, Michelle, Ellen Hock, et al., "Navy Mothers Experiencing and Not Experiencing Deployment: Reasons for Staying in or Leaving the Military," *Military Psychology,* Vol. 13, No. 1, 2001, pp. 56–71.

Kirby, Sheila Nataraj, and Scott Naftel, *The Effect of Mobilization on Retention of Enlisted Reservists After Operation Desert Shield/Storm,* Santa Monica, Calif.: RAND, MR-943-OSD, 1998.

Kirmeyer, Sandra, and Thomas Dougherty, "Work Load, Tension, and Coping: Moderating Effects of Supervisor Support," *Personnel Psychology,* Vol. 41, No. 1, Spring 1988, pp. 125–139.

Klein, Gary, "The Effects of Acute Stressors on Decision-Making," in James Driskell and Eduardo Salas, eds., *Stress and Human Performance,* Mahwah, N.J.: Lawrence Erlbaum Associates, 1996, pp. 49–88.

Kozlowksi, Steve, "Training and Developing Adaptive Teams: Theory, Principles, and Research," in Janis Cannon-Bowers and Eduardo Salas, eds., *Making Decisions Under Stress,* Washington, D.C.: American Psychological Association, 1998, pp. 115–153.

Laibson, David, Samuel McClure, George Loewenstein, and Jonathan Cohen, "Separate Neural Systems Value Immediate and Delayed Monetary Rewards," *Science,* Vol. 306, October 15, 2004. Available online at http://www.sciencemag.org; last accessed October 9, 2005.

Lakhani, Hyder, "Reenlistment Intentions of Citizen Soldiers in the U.S. Army," *Armed Forces & Society,* Vol. 22, No. 1, Fall 1995, pp.117–130.

Lakhani, Hyder, and Elissa T. Abod, "The Effectiveness of Economic Incentives for Career Commitment of Peacekeepers in the Sinai," *Armed Forces & Society,* Vol. 25, No. 3, Spring 1997, pp. 391–414.

Lakhani, Hyder, and S. Fugita, "Reserve/Guard Retention: Moonlighting or Patriotism?" *Military Psychology,* Vol. 5, No. 2, 1993, pp. 113–125.

Larsen, Rolf, "Decision-Making by Military Students Under Extreme Stress," *Military Psychology,* Vol. 13, No. 2, 2001, pp. 89–92.

Lazarus, R., and S. Folkman, "Stress, Appraisal, and Coping," *Journal of Health and Social Behavior,* Vol. 19, 1984, pp. 2–21.

Lee, Thomas W., Terence R. Mitchell, Brooks, C. Holtom, Linda S. McDaniel, and John W. Hill, "The Unfolding Model of Voluntary Turnover: A Replication and Extension," *Academy of Management Journal,* Vol. 42, No. 4, 1999, pp. 450–462.

Leitch, Matthew, "A New Approach to Stress Management: Why Uncertainty Causes Stress, and How to Stop It," February 13, 2003. Available online at http://www.managedluck.co.uk/stress/; accessed December 7, 2004.

Little, Roger W., "The Military Family," *Handbook of Military Institutions,* Beverly Hills, Calif.: Sage, 1971, pp. 247–270.

Litz, B., L. King, D. King, S. Orsillo, and M. Friedman, "Posttraumatic Stress Disorder Associated with Peacekeeping Duty in Somalia for US Military Personnel," *American Journal of Psychiatry,* Vol. 154, 1997a, pp. 178–184.

———, "Warriors as Peacekeepers: Features of the Somali Experience and PTSD," *Journal of Consult Clinician Psychology,* 1997b, pp. 1001–1009.

Lott, A. J., and B. E. Lott, "Group Cohesiveness as Interpersonal Attraction: A Review of Relationships with Antecedent and Consequent Variables," *Psychological Bulletin,* Vol. 64, 1965, pp. 259–309.

Lynn, Adam, "A Support Group for Soldiers," *Tacoma News Tribune,* August 11, 2004.

MacCoun, Robert, "What Is Known About Unit Cohesion and Military Performance," in Bernard Rostker, Scott A. Harris, James P. Kahan, et al., *Sexual Orientation and U.S. Military Personnel Policy, Options, and Assessment,* Santa Monica, Calif.: RAND, MR-323-OSD, 1993.

Mace, R., and L. Carroll, "The Control of Anxiety in Sport: Stress Inoculation Training Prior to Abseiling," *International Journal of Sport Psychology,* Vol. 16, 1985, pp. 165–175.

Mandler, George, "Thought, Memory, and Learning: Effects of Emotional Stress," in Leo Goldberger and Shlomo Breznitz, eds., *The Handbook of Stress,* 2nd Ed., New York: The Free Press, 1993.

Marshall, T., et al., "A Randomized Controlled Trial of the Effect of Anticipation of a Blood Test on Blood Pressure," *Journal of Human Hypertension,* Vol. 16, 2002, pp. 621–625.

Martz, Ron, "Georgia Air Guard Numbers Stable," *Atlanta Journal-Constitution,* August 14, 2004, p. A13.

Maslach, Christina, Wilmar Schaufeli, and Michael Leiter, "Job Burnout," *Annual Review of Psychology,* 2001.

Maurer, Kevin, "Exercises Give Soldiers Realistic Training Experience," *Fayetteville Observer,* August 12, 2004.

———, "Stress Afflicts Bragg Troops," *Fayetteville Observer,* August 10, 2004.

McCarroll, J., R. Ursano, C. Fullerton, "Symptoms of Posttraumatic Stress Disorder Following Recovery of War Dead," *American Journal of Psychiatry,* Vol. 150, 1993, pp. 1875–1877.

McClure, P., and W. Broughton, *Military Community Cohesion,* Scranton, Penn.: Marywood University, MFI Technical Report 98-4, 1988.

McGrath, J., "Stress and Behavior in Organizations," in M. Dunnette, ed., *Handbook of Industrial and Organizational Psychology, Volume 3,* 2nd Ed., Chicago, Ill.: Rand MacNally, 1976, pp. 1351–1395.

McLemore, David, "Army Program Aims to Ease Stressed Out Soldiers' Return," *Dallas Morning News,* March 15, 2004.

McLeod, Peter, "A Dual Task Modality Effect: Support for Multiprocessor Models of Attention," *Quarterly Journal of Experimental Psychology,* Vol. 29, No. 4, November 1977, pp. 651–667.

McNally, Richard, "Revulsion to War," *Los Angeles Times,* July 8, 2004.

Meglino, B., "Stress and Performance: Are They Always Compatible?" *Supervisory Management,* Vol. 22, No. 3, 1977, pp. 2–12.

Milgram, N., R. Orenstien, and E. Zafrir, "Stressors, Personal Resources, and Social Supports in Military Performance During Wartime," *Military Sociology,* Vol. 1, No. 4, 1989, pp. 185–199.

Miller, Laura L., "Do Soldiers Hate Peacekeeping? The Case of Preventive Diplomacy Operations in Macedonia," *Armed Forces & Society,* Vol. 23, No. 3, Spring 1997, pp. 415–450.

Miller, Laura L., and Charles Moskos, "Humanitarians or Warriors? Race, Gender, and Combat Status in Operation Restore Hope," *Armed Forces & Society,* Vol. 21, No. 4, Summer 1995, pp. 615–637.

Mitchell, Terence R., Brooks C. Holtom, Thomas W. Lee, Chris J. Sablynski, and Miriam Erez, "Why People Stay: Using Job Embeddedness to Predict Voluntary Turnover," *Academy of Management Journal,* Vol. 44, No. 6, 2001, pp. 1102–1121.

Mohr, D., R. Holzbach, and R. Morrison, *Surface Warfare Junior Officer Retention: Spouses' Influence on Career Decisions,* San Diego, Calif.: Navy Personnel Research and Development Center, NPRDC Technical Report 81-17, 1981.

Moore, Brenda, "The Propensity of Junior Enlisted Personnel to Remain in Today's Military," *Armed Forces & Society,* Vol. 28, No. 2, Winter 2002, pp. 257–278.

Moskos, Charles C., *The American Enlisted Man,* New York: Russell Sage Foundation, 1970.

———, *Peace Soldiers,* Chicago, Ill.: University of Chicago Press, 1976.

Moskos, Charles C., and Frank R. Wood, eds., *The Military: More Than Just a Job?* Washington, D.C.: Pergamon-Brassey's International Defense Publishers, Inc., 1988.

Mueller, Charles W., "Commitment to Nested Organizational Units: Some Basic Principles and Preliminary Findings," *Social Psychology Quarterly,* Vol. 62, No. 4, 1999, pp. 325–346.

Mullen, B., and C. Cooper, "The Relation between Group Cohesiveness and Performance: An Integration," Syracuse, N.Y.: Syracuse University, Department of Psychology, unpublished manuscript, 1993.

Muse, Lori, Stanley Harris, and Hubert Feild, "Has the Inverted-U Theory of Stress and Job Performance Had a Fair Test?" *Human Performance,* Vol. 16, No. 4, September 2003, pp. 349–364.

Oliver, L. W., *Cohesion Research: Conceptual and Methodological Issues,* Alexandria, Va.: U.S. Army Research Institute for Behavioral and Social Sciences, 1990.

"Operation Enduring Freedom–Afghanistan." Available online at http://www.globalsecurity.org/military/ops/enduring-freedom.htm; accessed November 29, 2004.

Orthner, D., *Families in Blue: Implications of a Study of Married and Single Parent Families in the US Air Force,* Greensboro, N.C.: Family Research and Analysis, USAF Contract F03360-79-C-0423, 1980.

Pearson, David, and Richard Thackray, "Consistency of Performance Change and Autonomic Response as a Function of Expressed Attitude Toward a Specific Stress Situation," *Psychophysiology,* Vol. 6, No. 5, 1970, pp. 561–568.

Pedrotti, Kay, "Program Will Help Army Families Cope," *Atlanta Journal–Constitution,* July 8, 2004.

Pleck, J. H., "Paternal Involvement: Levels, Sources, and Consequences," in M. E. Lamb, ed., *The Role of the Father in Child Development,* New York: Wiley, 1997, pp. 66–103.

Rakoff, Stuart H., Janet D. Griffith, and Gary A. Zarkin, *Models of Soldier Retention,* Alexandria, Va.: U.S. Army Research Institute for the Behavioral and Social Sciences, June 1994.

Reed, Brian J., and David R. Segal, "The Impact of Multiple Deployments on Soldiers' Peacekeeping Attitudes, Morale, and Retention," *Armed Forces & Society,* Vol. 27, No. 1, Fall 2000, pp. 57–78.

Ricks, Thomas, "US Army Changed by Iraq, but for Better or Worse?" *Washington Post,* July 16, 2004, p. A10.

Roeder, Tom, "Carson Soldiers Readjusting Well," *Colorado Springs Gazette,* July 1, 2004, p. 1.

Rogers, Rick, "Returning Marines Face New Battle at Home," *San Diego Union Tribune,* July 1, 2004.

Rosen, Leora, and Doris Briley Durand, "The Family Factor and Retention Among Married Soldiers Deployed in Operation Desert Storm," *Military Psychology,* Vol. 7, No. 4, 1995, pp. 221–234.

Sanders, A., "Towards a Model for Stress and Human Performance," *Acta Psychologica,* Vol. 53, 1983, pp. 61–97.

Sarkesian, Sam C., ed., *Combat Effectiveness: Cohesion, Stress, and the Volunteer Military,* Beverly Hills, Calif.: Sage, 1980.

Saunders, Teri, et al., "The Effects of Stress Inoculation Training on Anxiety and Performance," *Journal of Occupational Health Psychology,* Vol. 1, No. 2, April 1996, pp. 170–186.

Scarborough, Rowan, "Army Divisions Hit Re-Up Targets," *Washington Times,* April 2, 2004, p. 1.

———, "Stressed Troops Turn to Smokes, Alcohol, Prayer," *Washington Times,* March 9, 2004, p. 3.

Scharnberg, Kirsten, "Stresses of Battle Hit Female GIs Hard: VA Study Hopes to Find Treatment for Disorder," *Chicago Tribune,* March 20, 2005. Available online at http://www.chicagotribune .com/news/nationworld/chi-0503200512mar20,1,7627407.story?coll=chi-newsnationworld-hed&ctrack=1&cset=true; accessed April 6, 2005.

Schmitt, Eric, and Thom Shanker, "Army to Call Up Recruits Earlier," *The New York Times,* July 22, 2004.

Schumm, Walter R., D. Bruce Bell, Morten G. Ender, and Rose E. Rice, "Expectations, Use and Evaluation of Communication Media Among Deployed Peacekeepers," *Armed Forces & Society,* Vol. 30, No. 4, Spring 2004, pp. 649–662.

Scully, Megan, "US Army Adapts Training to Reflect Threats in Iraq," DefenseNews.com, May 20, 2004.

Segal, David, Theodore Furukawa, and Jerry Lindh, "Light Infantry as Peacekeepers in the Sinai," *Armed Forces & Society,* Vol. 16, No. 3, Spring 1990, pp. 385–403.

Segal, David, David Rohall, Joseph Jones, and Angela Manos, "Meeting the Missions of the 1990s with a Downsized Force: Human Resource Management Lessons from the Deployment of PATRIOT Missile Units to Korea," *Military Psychology,* Vol.11, No. 2, 1999, pp. 149–167.

Segal, David, and Mady Wechsler Segal, *Peacekeepers and Their Wives,* Westport, Conn.: Greenwood Press, 1993.

Segal, Mady Wechsler, "The Military and the Family as Greedy Institutions," in Charles C. Moskos and Frank R. Wood, eds., *The Military: More Than Just a Job?* Washington, D.C.: Pergamon-Brassey's International Defense Publishers, Inc., 1988, pp. 79–98.

Segal, Mady Wechsler, and Jesse J. Harris, *What We Know About Army Families,* Alexandria, Va.: U.S. Army Research Institute for the Behavioral and Social Sciences, Special Report 21, 1993.

Selye, Hans, *The Stress of Life,* New York: McGraw-Hill, 1956.

———, *Stress Without Distress,* New York: J. P. Lippicott Company, 1975.

Serfaty, Daniel, Elliot Entin, and Joan Johnston, "Team Coordination Training," in Janis Cannon-Bowers and Eduardo Salas, eds., *Making Decisions Under Stress,* Washington D.C.: American Psychological Association, 1998, pp. 221–245.

Seymour, D., and K. Black, "Stress in Primary Care Patients," in F. DeGruy III et al., eds., *20 Common Problems in Behavioral Health,* New York: McGraw-Hill, 2002, pp. 65–87.

Shaham, Yavin, Jerome Singer, and Monica Schaeffer, "Stability/Instability of Cognitive Strategies Across Tasks Determine Whether Stress Will Affect Judgmental Processes," *Journal of Applied Psychology,* Vol. 22, No. 9, 1992, pp. 691–713.

Shanker, Thom, "Army Pushes a Sweeping Overhaul of Basic Training," *The New York Times,* August 4, 2004.

———, "Military Plans to Call Up Soldiers Who Left Service," *The New York Times,* June 30, 2004.

Sheehy, Richard, and John Horan, "Effects of Stress Inoculation Training for 1st Year Law Students," *International Journal of Stress Management,* Vol. 11, No. 4, February 2004, pp. 41–55.

Shields, Patricia, "A New Paradigm for Military Policy: Socioeconomics," *Armed Forces & Society,* Vol. 19, Summer 1993, pp. 511–531.

Shils, Edward A., and Morris Janowitz, "Cohesion and Disintegration in the Wehrmacht in World War II," *Public Opinion Quarterly,* Vol. 12, Summer 1948, pp. 280–315.

Srivastava, A., and A. Krishna, "A Test of Inverted 'U'-Hypothesis of Stress Performance Relationship in the Industrial Context," *Psychological Studies,* Vol. 34, 1991, pp. 34–38.

Staw, R., L. Sandelands, and J. Dutton, "Threat-Rigidity Effects in Organizational Behavior: A Multi-Level Analysis," *Administrative Quarterly,* No. 26, 1981, pp. 501–524.

Stouffer, Samuel A., Arthur A. Lumsdaine, Marion Harper Lumsdaine, Robin M. Williams, Jr., M. Brewster Smith, Irving L. Janis, Shirley A. Star, and Leonard S. Cottrell, Jr., *Studies in Social Psychology in World War II: Volume 2, The American Soldier: Combat and Its Aftermath,* Princeton, N.J.: Princeton University Press, 1949.

Stouffer, Samuel A., Edward A. Suchman, Leland C. DeVinney, Shirley A. Star, and Robin M. Williams, Jr., *Studies in Social Psychology in World War II: Volume 1, The American Soldier: Adjustment During Army Life,* Princeton, N.J.: Princeton University Press, 1949.

Sweeney, G., and J. Horan, "Separate and Combined Effects of Cue-Controlled Relaxation and Cognitive Restructuring in the Treatment of Musical Performance Anxiety," *Journal of Counseling Psychology,* Vol. 29, 1982, pp. 486–497.

Teplitzky, Martha, Shelley Thomas, and Glenda Nogami, *Dual Army Career Officers: Job Attitudes and Career Intentions of Male and Female Officers,* Alexandria, Va.: U.S. Army Research Institute for the Behavioral and Social Sciences, ARI Technical Report 805, 1988.

Timms, Ed, "Trained to Fight, Soldiers Adapt to New Duties," *Dallas Morning News,* June 22, 2004.

Tyson, Ann Scott, "Army Having Difficulty Meeting Goals in Recruiting: Fewer Enlistees Are in Pipeline; Many Being Rushed into Service," *Washington Post,* February 21, 2005a, p. A1.

———, "Suicides in Marine Corps Rise by 29%: Fast Pace of Operations Are Believed to Contribute," *The Washington Post,* February 25, 2005b, p. A19.

"US Casualty Status—Operation Iraqi Freedom, Operation Enduring Freedom." Available online at http://www.defenselink.mil/news/casualty.pdf; accessed November 29, 2004.

Vroom, V., *Work and Motivation,* New York: Wiley Press, 1964.

Warner, John, and Bruce Simon, *An Empirical Analysis of Pay and Navy Enlisted Retention in the AVF: Preliminary Results,* Alexandria, Va.: Center for Naval Analyses, Memorandum 79-1878, December 1979.

Weiss, Howard M., Shelley M. MacDermid, Rachelle Strauss, Katherine E. Kurek, Benjamin Le, and David Robbins, *Retention in the Armed Forces: Past Approaches and New Research Directions,* Lafayette, Ind.: Purdue University, Military Family Research Institute, March 2003.

Welch, William M., "Trauma of Iraq War Haunting Thousands Returning Home: A New Generation of Vets Is Seeking Help for Stress Disorder," *USA Today,* February 28, 2005, p. 1.

Wong, Leonard, Paul Bliese, and Ronald Halverson, "Multiple Deployments: Do They Make a Difference?" Paper Presented at the Biennial Conference of the Inter-University Seminar on Armed Forces and Society, Baltimore, Md., October 1995.

Wood, David, "Army's Midcareer Leaders Are Bearing Up Under the Burden of War," Newhouse.com, June 2, 2004.

Wright, Kathleen, David Marlowe, and Robert Gifford, "Deployment Stress and Operation Desert Shield: Preparation for War," in Robert Ursano and Ann Norwood, eds., *Emotional Aftermath of the Persian Gulf War,* Washington, D.C.: American Psychiatric Press, 1996, pp. 283–313.

Yerkes, Robert, and John Dodson, "The Relation of Strength of Stimulus to Rapidity of Habit Formation," *Journal of Comparative Neurology and Psychology,* Vol. 18, 1908, pp. 459–482.

Zahn, Paula, "US Military Move on Fallujah; Battle Fatigue," *Paula Zahn Now,* CNN, April 27, 2004.

Zajonc, R., "Attitudinal Effects of Mere Exposure," *Journal of Personality and Social Psychology,* Vol. 9, 1968, pp. 1–27.

Zaroya, Greg, "For Combat-Weary Marines, Each Stint Adds to the Strain," *USA Today,* July 29, 2005.